The Fast Guide to Cubase

Simon Millward

PC Publishing

PC Publishing
Export House
130 Vale Road
Kent TN9 1SP
UK

Tel 01732 770893
Fax 01732 770268
email pcp@cix.compulink.co.uk
web site http://www.pc-pubs.demon.co.uk

First published 1997

© PC Publishing

ISBN 1 870775 49 X

British Library Cataloguing in Publication Data
A catalogue record for this book is available from the British Library

Printed in Great Britain by Bell and Bain, Glasgow

Introduction

Welcome to the *Fast Guide to Cubase*. This book aims to give users a solid grounding in the use of Steinberg's flagship software sequencer package. It serves as a handy quick reference and provides a fast way into the essentials of MIDI sequencing using Cubase. The features described here are relevant to all Cubase users and most examples given are accurate for the three computer platforms for which the software is available (Atari/CLab Falcon, Macintosh and PC). This guide has been prepared using different versions of Cubase on various platforms. Occasionally, there may be superficial differences between the examples given and the reader's own software version and platform.

Before we begin in earnest let's take some time to be aware of one of the main stumbling blocks in the use of a MIDI based sequencer: the tendency to become too pre-occupied with the technical details of the system and to forget that the object of the exercise was to achieve a musical result. Many readers will have already witnessed the scene in the recording studio when the musicians wait for hours on end while the programmer grapples with all kinds of obscure parameters in the quest for musical perfection.

Rule number 1, in this book, is quite philosophical : musical perfection does not exist and, even if it did, a MIDI sequencer should not be used to search for it! As we shall see, some level of technical involvement is inevitable but the secret is to know the limits of the software and to be properly equipped before taking the plunge. Luckily, with Cubase the user can, to some extent, choose how deeply he/she wishes to go and the creators, to their credit, have designed a user interface which can be adapted to each individual's needs.

It has been assumed that readers are already reasonably experienced with their computer platform, so the text concentrates on the operational aspects of the software. For the general setting up of the computer and related hardware, please refer to the relevant user manuals and the Cubase manual.

This book is the result of years of experience, in recording studios and at home, with the various versions of Steinberg Cubase. Chapters 1 and 2 provide an overview of the Cubase system in general and a guide to the main working areas of the program. Chapter 3 outlines the major functions and options available in the menus and gives practical guidance on how best to use them. Chapter 4 provides an introduction to Score Edit, a truly major feature of the program, with tutorials suggesting how to achieve the best results. Chapter 5 provides an advanced practical tutorial on Logical Edit and, at the same time, gives the reader an insight into the theory of MIDI and the manipulation of data in general. A glossary is provided at the end of the book to help those who are unfamiliar with the terminology of MIDI, sequencers and music technology.

Contents

Acknowledgements

My thanks to Niels Larsen, Graeme Down and the Steinberg Team at Harman Audio, Debbie Poyser, Matt Bell and the staff at *Sound on Sound* magazine, and Vic Lennard.

And to my friends and family whose support helped make this book possible.

System overview and the Arrange window

Cubase is a comprehensive music recording and publishing software package. Its wide range of features could be viewed as a virtual 'universe' encompassing the needs of almost every user (see Figure 1.1).

The centre of activity is the 'Arrange Window', the 'sun' of the system. This is the default page which appears when Cubase is first loaded, and most users travel back and forth from here to other parts of the program. The Arrange window is where recorded music, in the form of graphic blocks (Parts), can be viewed in various resolutions, re-arranged, copied, deleted, repeated etc., much like the actions of a word processor.

Figure 1.1 The Cubase universe – rather like the solar system with the Arrange Window as the Sun and the editors as the planets

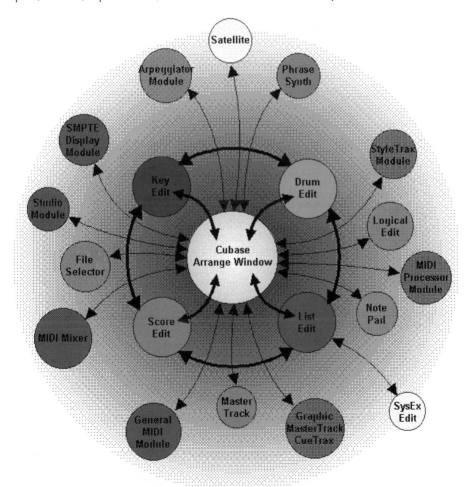

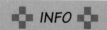
Moving outwards from the arrange 'planet' we find Key, List, Drum and Score edit. These are accessible via the Edit menu or with keyboard commands. Once music has been recorded in the Arrange window it may be looked at in fine detail in the editors. Each editor has been styled to present the notes, (or other data), in its own particular way.

Edit screens

Key edit

Key edit is a piano roll style editor, showing notes displayed on a grid where the horizontal axis represents time (displayed as bars, beats and fractions of a beat) and the vertical axis represents pitch (displayed as a piano keyboard).

List edit

List edit shows notes (and any other MIDI events) displayed as a written list of data accompanied by a time based graphic representation of events.

Drum edit

Drum edit, as the name implies, shows drum style events on a grid, where the horizontal axis represents time, and the vertical axis represents the names of the separate instruments of a drum kit or percussion setup.

Score edit

Score edit shows all note data as musical notation.

Logical edit

Going further out from the centre we come to Logical edit. Although appearing rather unfriendly, Logical edit provides an extremely useful interface whereby mathematical operations can be performed upon musical and other data. This can save enormous amounts of time.

Travelling further

Travelling on the same orbit we come to the Note Pad, which is precisely that: a facility where you can type in reminders and written notes. Moving round further we find the Mastertrack, a tempo and time signature manager. Next is the File Selector, which is an updated interface for disk operations (available on the Atari/Falcon version).

Modules

As implied by the term module, these parts of the program can be hooked on, when required, or jettisoned when not in use, so as to free up precious RAM memory. In the Atari/Falcon version, Score edit is a module and need only be loaded by those users requiring score facilities. The Mac/PC versions feature Score edit, the General MIDI editor, the Graphic Master track (CueTrax), the MIDI Mixer and the Interactive Phrase Synthesizer (IPS) as standard parts of the program, depending on which version is being used.

Modules include varying combinations of the following: the MIDI Mixer, a facility where custom designed MIDI processing tools can be assembled; the IPS (Interactive Phrase Synthesizer), a kind of real time re-processing plant for musical sequences; the MIDI Processor, which can produce MIDI delays and echo effects; the Arpeggiator, for the creation of various kinds of arpeggios; the Studio Module, for the editing of sounds and the detailed management of the MIDI system in use; CueTrax, a graphic version of Cubase's Mastertrack; the General MIDI Module, for the selection of GM sounds by name rather than program number; StyleTrax, an auto accompaniment program; and the SMPTE Display Module, a large digit Time Code display (Mac/PC versions only).

Satellite and SysEx editor module

In the outer reaches of the planetary system we find Satellite, a free accessory with earlier Atari versions of Cubase providing bank loading, saving and sound editing functions. This has been superseded by the Studio Module which fulfils the same functions more comprehensively. On the same orbit there is the SysEx editor module, an offshoot of the List editor, where manufacturer-specific data can be viewed and edited (Atari/Falcon version only). The SysEx editor is, in fact, another module but is only accessible from within List edit.

Moving around in Cubase

Figure 1.1 also displays the principal routes of travel between the different parts of the system. The user may leave the Arrange window and view the music in any one of the four main editors, or in one editor after the other or, if the need arises, in all at the same time. Going back and forth between the Arrange window and any one of the editors, or between different editors, tend to be the most popular routes of travel in the routine recording and editing of a piece of music. Note that music need not be recorded exclusively in the Arrange window; it can also be implemented while in any one of the main editors.

Most menu items are accessible from almost anywhere in the system but the saving and loading of song files and arrangements must usually be performed while in the Arrange window. Other parts of the system, such as the modules, are readily accessible once they have been made active. However, at this stage, they may seem somewhat obscure since they are often for the specialised processing or manipulation of data other than the music itself.

That gives a reasonable overview of the Cubase system. But why this rather elaborate analogy to a solar system? Well, scientists got an awful lot in perspective when they realised that the Earth and other planets revolved around the Sun, rather than vice versa. Similarly, musicians and programmers will understand Cubase more easily when they have a clear idea of how the whole system is put together.

However, although it is important for you to have this overview, this book will not be covering the entire range of the program's features. It will, however, provide enough detail so that anybody would be able to quickly find their way around the system and, equipped with the essential skills, go on to create the music of their choice.

Testing the controls

And now onto some of those details. Rather than plunge straight into recording some music, let's take some time to understand the ways of manipulating the system on the surface. Many users have a tendency to plunge too deeply, too soon and to become totally mouse bound. Remember that there are a substantial number of keyboard commands which make moving around the system faster and easier.

It has been assumed that all users know how to load up Cubase. If not, then please read the Cubase manual which will give you the details required. It is important that your system is installed with the correct driver(s) for your particular MIDI interface/sound card or other hardware.

On the Atari/Falcon, Cubase supports a range of commonly available hardware devices and, on the PC, all MIDI interfaces which come with a windows Multimedia driver are supported. The PC drivers are installed using the windows Control Panel, or separate installation software, and provide communication between the MIDI interface and the Multimedia Extensions (MME) part of windows. Cubase is then able to communicate with MME via its own driver.

So, load up the software, as usual, and the Arrange window should appear on the computer screen with various default settings. Now let's use some of those keyboard commands to move around the system. We are not following any particular logic here, but just becoming familiar with the controls. It's rather like learning to drive a car – it's a good idea to get the feel of the controls before actually going out on the road. The tables show some of the most important keyboard commands.

Numeric keypad shortcuts

Numeric keypad	Function
*	record
Enter	play/continue
0 or spacebar	first time – stop
	second time – go to left locator
	third time – go to bar 1.1.0
(or PgDn	rewind
) or PgUp	fast forward
1	go to left locator
2	go to right locator
/	cycle on/off
+	increase tempo
–	decrease tempo

Computer keyboard shortcuts

Computer keybd	Function
ctrl + O	open (load) file
ctrl + S	save file
ctrl + Q	quit program
ctrl + E	Key edit
ctrl + G	List edit
ctrl + D	Drum edit
ctrl + R	Score edit
ctrl + L	Logical edit
ctrl + F	MIDI mixer
ctrl + B	Note Pad
ctrl + H	transpose/velocity
ctrl + M	open the Master Track
ctrl + T	create a new Track
ctrl + P	create a new Part
ctrl + K	repeat
ctrl + X	cut
ctrl + C	copy
ctrl + V	paste
alt(+ ctrl) + I	open/close the Inspector
alt(+ ctrl) + P	move locators to start and end points of the selected Part
alt(+ ctrl) + N	open name entry box of the currently selected Track
G	horizontal zoom in
H	horizontal zoom out
shift + G	vertical zoom in
shift + H	vertical zoom out
S	solo on/off
D	overdub/replace record mode
I	punch in on/off
O	punch out on/off
C	metronome click on/off
M	Master Track active/inactive
delete	delete selection
clr/home	move song position pointer to start of current window
esc	cancel (or leave a dialogue box)

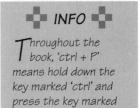

So, without attempting to achieve anything musically constructive, let's try some of the control commands on the computer keyboard. Select ctrl + P to create a new blank 'Part' in the Arrange window between the left and right locators (two small boxes in the bar display marked L and R, Figures 1.3 and 1.4). 'Parts' are graphic blocks which appear in the working area to the right of the Track list. They would usually contain musical data but they may also be empty, as in this case. Then try ctrl + E followed by ctrl + L, which will normally open up Key edit followed by Logical edit. Pressing the escape key will exit from each editor and take you back to the Arrange window. Try the other 'ctrl plus a key' commands to move around the system.

Other immediately useful key commands include the G and H keys which zoom in or out in the Arrange and edit windows, the C key for turning the guide click on and off, the S key for soloing the selected Track and the + and - keys of the numeric keypad to change the tempo.

The numeric keypad

The numeric keypad may be viewed as a kind of tape recorder remote control. Although all the controls are obviously already available to the mouse on the computer screen, their repetition on the keypad provides a handy alternative. Users will also find this indispensable after having used the hide transport option in the Windows menu.

The mouse

Let's now go on to use the mouse. The mouse is most useful for all the graphic elements of the system, such as dragging objects around the screen, changing values, using tools and fine editing in the editors. But it's also the preferred method of opening up what are effectively the contents pages of the system: the menus. These are found under various headings at the top of the computer screen.

The menus

Figure 1.2 shows all the menu contents at once (note that the menus will vary according to version and platform). It is immediately apparent from here that Cubase is extremely comprehensive. Some of the most important elements include the metronome and MIDI Setup options, the various editors, the quantize functions, the copy, repeat and transposition functions and, of course, the file save and load functions. Most of the important menu items will be dealt with during the course of the book but, before we jump too far ahead, let's go back to what actually happened when we first loaded Cubase into the computer.

Those of you who have managed to read the manual thoroughly will know that Cubase appears on the screen after having auto loaded any DEF files found on the disk (DEF.ALL, DEF.ARR, DEF.SET etc.). These are Definition files which contain the user preferences for the setup and general handling of the system when Cubase is booted up, including the appearance and contents of the Arrange window and editors. It might have seemed logical to set up a Definition file before recording any music

File	Edit	Structure	Functions	Options	Modules	Score	Windows
New	Undo	Create Track	Over Quantize	Chase Events	Setup...	Page Mode	Cascade
Open...	Cut	Global Cut	Note On Quantize	Multirecord		Layout Layer only	Tile
Close	Copy	Global Insert	Iterative Quantize	Part Appearance	MIDI Processor	Staff Settings...	Stack
Save Song	Paste	Global Split	Analytic Quantize	Part Background...	SMPTE Display	Staff Presets	Tile Editors
Save Arrange	Delete Track	Copy Range	Groove Quantize	Follow Song	AVI Monitor	Staff Functions	Stack Editors
Save As...	Select	Remix		Record Tempo / Mut		Symbol Palettes	Hide Transport
Revert to Sav	Copy to Phrase	Mix Down	Undo Quantize			Note Head Shape	def.arr
			Freeze Quantize	MIDI Setup...			
Import MIDI	Edit	Create Part	Setup Grooves...	MIDI Filter...		Text Settings...	
Export MIDI	List	Repeat...		Input Transformer...			
	Drum	Cut Events	Logical	Metronome...		Format	
Print & Page	Score		Freeze PP	Synchronization...		Auto Layout	
Print...	Mixer	Show Groups	Legato	Remote Control...			
	GM / GS Edit	Build Group...	Length Size	Setup Mixermaps...		Global Settings	
Preferences..	Get Info	Unpack Group	Fixed Length	Phrase Synth...		Export	
	Notepad		Delete Doubles				
Quit			Delete Cont. Data	Reset Devices		Force Update	
	Logical		Reduce Con Data				
	Mastertrack		Transpose / Veloc				

but before any meaningful definition files can be created you must have a good understanding of the essential features of the program.

Figure 1.2 The menus

Your first recording

Most first time users of Cubase cannot resist the temptation to put the sequencer into record mode and actually record some music, without ever having read the manual. This is certainly easy enough to do without any instructions and Cubase has, of course, been designed to make the recording process as trouble-free as possible. There is nothing to stop you pressing the Transport bar record button and attempting to record something and play it back without any knowledge of the parameters involved. However, it is not always certain that things will go according to plan.

This section demonstrates a simple approach to the recording process in order to avoid some of the grey areas which may arise for users impatient to make a trial recording.

TIP

Be careful with your locator positions! Accidentally placing the left locator to the wrong side of the right locator (or vice versa!) will cause Cubase to block any attempt at recording.

1 Connect your MIDI keyboard

You must first ensure that a MIDI keyboard, (or other input source), has its MIDI Out connected to the MIDI In of the computer's MIDI interface. This can be verified by checking the 'IN' MIDI activity indicator on the Transport bar while playing the MIDI keyboard. Reasons for no activity indication include an interface that has been wrongly installed, an inappropriate device selection in the Output column of the Arrange window (see below) or a MIDI cable connected incorrectly. Ensure also that the MIDI Out of the computer's MIDI interface is connected to the MIDI In of the keyboard (see Figure 1.5 later in this chapter).

2 Set Output column

The current track should have its Output column set to an output port of the MIDI interface/device in use. (The Output column is revealed by clicking and dragging on the Arrange window split point and pulling the cur-

tain to the right). This could be one of many devices with such names as, for example, MPU401, AWE32, and Voyetra etc. for the PC or Atari and Xport for the Atari/Falcon. An appropriate MIDI channel should also be selected in the channel column (chn).

3 Activate MIDI Thru

On all but the very rarest of occasions the MIDI thru of Cubase should be made active . This is found in the MIDI setup dialogue of the options menu and should be ticked. This ensures that any MIDI data received at the MIDI In of Cubase is echoed or through put to the MIDI Out.

4 Set Metronome

Before recording anything, ensure that there is an appropriate precount and guide click by adjusting the status of the metronome found in the Options menu. Try ticking 'precount', 'prerecord', 'beep' and 'MIDI click' and set a precount of two bars. Set the MIDI click Channel and Output to an appropriate drum or percussion sound source if there is one available. (MIDI channel 10 is the standard MIDI channel for drums and percussion sounds and the selection of C#1 as the note for a MIDI click is the standard position for a rimshot sound). Click on OK to leave the Metronome dialogue.

5 Activate Click

Ensure that Click is activated and the tempo adjusted to the desired setting on the Transport bar. This provides a guide click from the computer's speaker or from a MIDI instrument, as set above. Leave all other Transport bar settings in their default positions.

6 Start recording

To record, select the record button on the Transport bar. Cubase will output a two bar count, as set in the metronome, before recording commences from the left locator position (a small box marked with an L found in the position bar above the Part Display). Anything played on the keyboard will be recorded by Cubase.

7 Stop recording

Stop recording by selecting the stop button on the Transport bar. At this moment a graphic strip will appear in the Arrange window display with the same name as the Track upon which it was recorded. This graphic strip is known as a 'Part' and it contains the music which has just been played.

8 Now play it back

To play back the performance simply rewind the song position using the rewind button, (or select the stop button a second time), and then select the play button.

The above eight steps should get you into recording with the minimum of fuss and you will notice that Cubase has been supplied with most of the parameters already sensibly set. Due to this fact, in most cases, only steps 6,7 and 8 are necessary to actually make the recording. Steps 1 to 5 ensure that you are aware of some of the parameters and preparation involved. Of course, once all the parameters have been set up successfully, steps 1 to 5 can be largely ignored in the routine recording process.

If you experience problems with this process you should, once again, ensure that:

- the MIDI cables are not faulty and have been connected correctly
- the MIDI interface has been correctly installed and is selected in the Arrange window Output column of the Track which is being recorded
- the MIDI Channel is appropriate in the Channel column
- any external equipment connected to the system is switched on and configured to receive MIDI information on the appropriate channel(s).

More aspects of the recording process are described in 'Recording details' below.

The Arrange window

The Arrange window (Figures 1.3 and 1.4) is divided into two sections by a moveable split point which can be pulled across to the left or right of the screen using a click and drag manoeuvre with the mouse. Pulling the curtain as far as possible to the left maximises the working area for the Arrangement, known as the Part Display. The Arrange window features time on the horizontal axis, represented as bars and beats, and on the vertical axis, Tracks, which are named in the Track column.

Figure 1.3 The Arrange window columns

Activity	Mute	Class	Track	Chn	Output	Instrument	T	Part Display
								Solo · · · Snap Bar · · · Quantize 16 · · · Mouse
A	M	C	Track	Chn	Output	Instrument	T	1 · · · · · 9 · · · ·
	●	♪	Guide	1	SMP 24 2	SY85		Verse
		♪	BD	10	SMP 24 1	SR16		BD BD BD A
		♪	HH	10	SMP 24 1	SR16		HH HH HH HH HH A
		♪	Snare	10	SMP 24 1	SR16		SN SN SN SN SN S
	●	♪	Shuffle A	10	SMP 24 1	SR16		sn sn sn s
		♪	HH Open	10	SMP 24 1	SR16		HH HH HH HH HH A
		♪	Snare 2	10	SMP 24 1	SR16		sn sn sn s
		＼	Percussion	9	SMP 24 2	S1000		
		♪	Highbell	1	SMP 24 2	SY85		
		♪	Bestbass	2	SMP 24 2	TX7		E E Bes
		♪	TX802 Perf	16	SMP 24 2	TX802		
		⤴	TX802 Edit		FE802			
		♪	Blip	10	SMP 24 1	SR16		sfx sfx
		♪	Voice FX	6	SMP 24 2	S1000		
	●	♪	SFX	3	SMP 24 2	Proteus	🔒	S
		♪	Piano	3	SMP 24 2	Proteus		
	●	♪	Testbass	2	SMP 24 2	TX7		

Activity
Mute
Class
Track
MIDI Channel
Output Port
Intsrument
Time Lock
Part Display

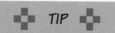
Pulling the curtain fully to the right reveals a number of columns which show the status of various settings governing each Track. These include:

- the activity column (A), showing the current MIDI activity of each Track in real time
- the mute column (M), where any number of Tracks may be muted
- the classification column (C), where Tracks can be designated as MIDI, drum, mix Tracks etc.,
- the Track column, where Tracks are named
- the MIDI channel column (Chn), where the MIDI channel for each Track may be chosen
- the Output column, where the MIDI port may be chosen
- the Instrument column, where any combination of the MIDI channel and output columns may be named
- the T column where Tracks may be 'time locked'.

Different combinations of the columns will be available depending on which version and platform is being used. Remember that the output column will contain only the output port names of the driver(s) you have installed with Cubase (see the Cubase Manual for installation details).

Some readers may have already noticed that there is also a separate mini-window to the left of the columns. This is known as the Inspector and is used to select sounds and change various parameters such as velocity, volume, delay and pitch transposition. The Inspector displays the parameters of the currently selected Track or Part in the Arrange window (the Track or Part which appears in black). It also contains the Track/Part name, the Instrument (if named), the Output port and the MIDI channel.

Figure 1.4 The Arrange
window, Inspector and
Transport bar

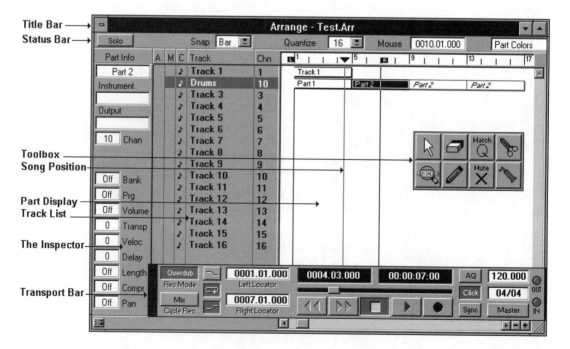

The Inspector can be shown or hidden by clicking on the small square shaped icon underneath it (see Chapter 3 for more details).

The current arrangement on screen can be one of several held in memory at the same time, (as found in the Arrange window list of the Windows menu). A new Arrange window may be created by selecting new in the File menu or pressing ctrl + N on the computer keyboard.

By clicking with the right mouse button, you may open the toolbox (see opened toolbox in Arrange window). This is for the manipulation and editing of Parts, and the main functions are as follows:

Pointer
The pointer is the default tool for the selection, moving and copying of Parts, and for the general manipulation of data anywhere on the screen.

Eraser
The eraser is for deleting Parts simply by clicking on one Part or by dragging over several.

Match Q
The match Q (match quantize) tool is used to impose the timing characteristics of one Part upon another by dragging and releasing a source Part over a target Part (see Chapter 3).

Scissors
the scissors are for splicing Parts into smaller portions. Parts will be split at the mouse position and according to the current Snap value.

Magnifying glass
The magnifying glass is for monitoring the contents of Parts by clicking and dragging it over any given Part with the left mouse button.

Pencil
The pencil is for lengthening and shortening Parts by grabbing and moving the end point of the Part. It may also be used to create new Parts anywhere on the Part display by clicking, holding and dragging in blank space.

Mute tool
The mute tool (you guessed it) is for muting Parts.

Glue tool
The glue tool is used to join two or more Parts to make one longer Part.

The Transport bar

The Transport bar, at the bottom of the screen, features a number of functions which have not yet been described. Apart from the obvious tape recorder style controls there are the following:

Record Mode selector

The Record Mode selector, for selecting whether Cubase adds to any existing music when recording ('Overdub mode') or overwrites it ('Replace mode').

Cycle button

The Cycle button, for cycling between the left and right locator positions.

Punch in and out buttons

The punch in and out buttons, for automatically dropping in and out of record mode at the left and right locator positions.

Note that Cubase always starts recording from the left locator position and when it is put into record mode the punch in button is automatically selected. However, if Cubase is rewound to a point some bars before the left locator and put into play with the punch in button manually selected, Cubase will drop in to record when it reaches the left locator position. If the punch out button has also been selected then Cubase will drop out of record at the right locator position, otherwise it will remain in record mode until you stop the sequencer.

Left and right locator positions

The left and right locator positions, showing the current positions of the locators.

Bar display

The bar display, showing the current position in bars, beats and fractions of a beat (ticks).

Time code display

The Time code display, showing the current song position in hours, minutes, seconds and frames.

Click on/off button

The Click on/off button, to toggle on or off the guide click (as set up in the Metronome dialogue).

Sync button

The Sync button, for synchronizing the sequencer to an external device such as a tape recorder.

Tempo and time

Displays showing the current tempo and time signature.

Master button

The Master button, for activating or de-activating the Mastertrack's tempo and time signature changes.

The Mac and PC versions also feature an Automatic quantize button (AQ), (found at the top of the Arrange window in the Atari/Falcon version), used to automatically quantize a performance as it is recorded, and a position slider (just below the bar and time position displays), for quickly moving to new song positions within the current arrangement. Note that the Atari/Falcon version's Transport bar includes a solo button which, on the Mac and PC, is found at the top of the Arrange window. This is used to solo the current Track.

All features may be updated or manipulated in some way using either the mouse or various computer keyboard commands. Remember that, normally, the left mouse button will decrease and the right mouse button will increase a value.

Recording details

And now, everybody breath a big sigh of relief – it's time to actually make a serious attempt at recording some music ! Well, almost ! As outlined in 'Your First recording' above, most readers will have Cubase connected to some kind of MIDI equipped synthesizer or piano keyboard and a network of MIDI devices, such as rackmount synth modules, drum machines or effects units (see Figure 1.5).

It is usually desirable for the MIDI data received, from the master keyboard, at the MIDI IN of the computer to be echoed to the MIDI OUT. So, open up the MIDI Setup dialogue box of the Options menu and ensure that MIDI THRU is active (ticked). Ensure also that SysEx and Aftertouch are filtered in the record and thru sections of the MIDI filter, also found in the Options menu. This will avoid recording any unnecessary data in this exercise.

It is also desirable, if possible, to set the master keyboard to LOCAL OFF. Local Off means that the keyboard is disconnected from the sound making part of the instrument. This avoids double notes and stops the

Figure 1.5 A typical MIDI network

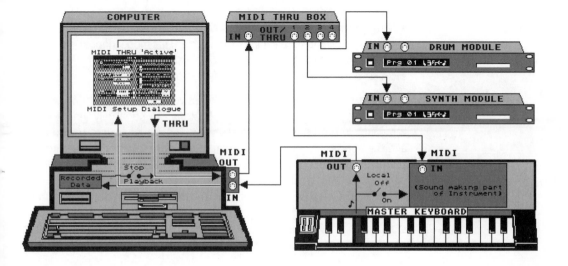

master keyboard sounding while other instruments in the network are being played via MIDI. It should now be possible to play any of the devices in the MIDI network by changing the MIDI channel in the channel column of the currently selected Track (using the left or right mouse buttons). Ensure also that the correct output device has been selected in the Output column.

Let's begin by recording a simple drum part on Track 2 (or a piano part if drums are not appropriate). To prepare the system for recording proceed as follows:

- Select the appropriate MIDI channel for the drum or percussion unit (or piano sound) in the system.
- Double click on the Track name and enter an appropriate name into the pop-up box.
- Set up the Metronome dialogue of the Options menu. As in 'Your First recording' above, this can be made to output a MIDI click to an appropriate sound, such as a rimshot, or can be set to give a guide click from the computer speaker. The count-in before recording commences is also adjustable.
- When back in the Arrange window turn the click on by pressing 'C' on the computer keyboard.
- Test the click and the tempo of Cubase by selecting the Transport play button with the mouse (or by using the 'enter' key on the numeric keypad). Adjust the tempo on the fly, if necessary, by clicking the left and right mouse buttons in the tempo box of the Transport bar or by clicking the + and - keys of the numeric keypad.
- Stop and return to bar 1.1.0 of the Arrange window. Set the left and right locators to bar positions 1.1.0 and 5.1.0 by clicking with the left and right mouse buttons in the position bar above the Arrangement area.
- Select Cycle in the Transport bar (using the mouse) or select the divide key (/) on the numeric keypad to put Cubase into cycle mode. Cubase will now cycle between the left and right locator positions in record or playback mode.
- Ensure that cycle record mode is set to 'mix' in order to be able to add to the recording on each lap of the cycle. This mode ignores the setting of the Record Mode selector.
- Ensure that Automatic Quantize (AQ) is off.

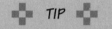
Cubase is now set to record and cycle between the left and right locators. In cycle mode the punch in and out buttons can be largely ignored since the punch in button is auto-selected when Cubase is put into record mode and the punch out point (the position of the right locator) is never actually reached since Cubase cycles back to the left locator position. Recording is de-activated only when Cubase is stopped manually.

You could also set up Cubase to record without cycle. In this mode recording begins from the left locator position and ends when Cubase is stopped or, if the punch out button has been activated, when the song position pointer reaches the right locator position.

Remember that, without cycle, the setting of the Record Mode selector must be taken into account. For most applications this would be set to 'Overdub', when recorded data will be added to any existing material already on the same Track. With the record mode selector set to 'Replace', any existing material on the Track will be overwritten, and as such this mode should be used with more caution.

We are now ready to actually record something. Some readers may consider this preparation far too much trouble just to put the system into the correct configuration to record some music. After all, recording onto a multitrack tape recorder is comparatively instantaneous. However, we must bear in mind that most of the steps described here were actually already sensibly set in the Definition files supplied with Cubase, so they are invariably set up only once, according to the preferences of each user. In addition, a sequencer of the power of Cubase has the capacity to fine tune and re-process recorded data beyond that of a multitrack tape recorder.

So, to record, proceed as follows.

Start recording

Click on the record button of the Transport bar or select the asterisk * on the numeric keypad. A pre-count will be heard according to what has been set in the metronome, and then the song position pointer should start to move.

Play something

Anything played on the keyboard will now be recorded into Cubase. Try recording something extremely simple using, for example, a bass drum and snare (or simple chords if a piano Part is being recorded). Cubase will cycle between the left and right locators (as set above), and the recording may be added to on each lap of the cycle.

Stop the recording

Stop the sequencer when recording is complete and a new Part will appear on the screen between the locators. Note that we are recording the Part as a normal MIDI Track (as indicated in the Track class column). Also note that a newly recorded Part will always appear in black, ready for further processing.

Quantize it?

If the new Part has been played extremely accurately it may not need any further attention, but a large number of users will want to quantize their work. Quantization is a form of timing correction which exists in various forms in the Functions menu of Cubase. Selecting Over quantize (or Q on the computer keyboard) will hard shift all notes to the nearest fraction of a beat, as set in the Quantize box above the Arrangement display. For example, if 16 is selected in the quantize box, Over quantize will shift each note in the Part onto the nearest 1/16 division of the bar. If a quantize method with more feel is required then try Iterative quantize (E on the computer keyboard). This shifts notes *towards* the nearest chosen

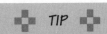

TIP

Many users prefer the cycle mode of recording since Cubase automatically remains within the segment of music which is being recorded upon without any further effort, and any newly recorded material can be instantly monitored on the next lap of the cycle. It is useful for continually adding to the material without dropping out of record and is particularly convenient for building up a rhythm pattern.

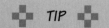

beat according to a strength percentage, which can be set in Edit Quantize. Iterative quantize tightens up parts that were loosely played but retains the feel of the playing. Note that there are several other quantize items in the Functions menu but these will be dealt with later, in Chapter 3.

Un-quantize needed?

Quantize the new Part using Over or Iterative quantize until it sounds musically correct. The quantize can be undone at any time using 'Undo quantize' in the Functions menu or pressing U on the computer keyboard. The Part will be returned to its original state. Parts recorded using Automatic quantize can also be returned to their unquantized state by pressing U. Remember that it is not desirable to have all the notes in all Parts occurring on exact divisions of the beat. This can result in music which is robotic and lifeless. Experienced MIDI musicians know that getting the right feel can make or break any piece of music.

Rename the new Part

Rename the Part by double clicking on it while holding Alt. Enter 'part 1' into the entry box.

Copy the Part

We could now immediately copy the Part. Click and hold the left mouse button on the Part while holding down Alt on the computer keyboard, (a small hand will appear), and drag the resulting outlined Part along the same Track to let go of it next to the original (using the same manoeuvre without holding down Alt would have simply moved the Part itself to the new position).

Rename the copy

Change the name of the copied Part to 'part 2'.

Create ghosts

Repeat 'part 2' twice using the repeat function of the structure menu, (ctrl + K on the computer keyboard). Simply enter a count of 2 and tick ghost copies. Two ghost Parts will appear on the Arrange display immediately after the original (see Figure 1.6). Ghost Parts are exact copies of one original and appear as grey Parts on the display. Any changes to the contents of the original 'part 2' will be replicated in the ghost Parts. 'part 1' remains a separate entity.

Save, save, save

Once you are satisfied with the result, use Save in the File menu to save the music to disk. Save as a Song file (.ALL extension) under an appropriate name. The file can now, of course, be recalled back into Cubase at any time using Open file.

Remember that the whole recording process, as outlined above, is a mere exercise, and you may, of course, adapt things to suit your own needs. To help clarify the basic recording process Figure 1.6 summarises the essential steps:

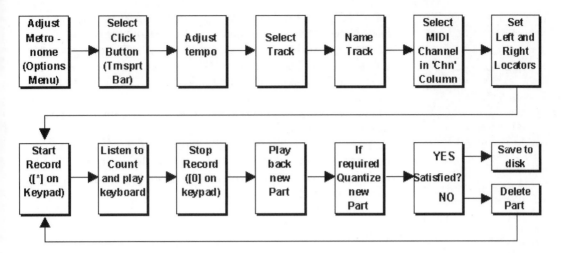

You will quickly find your own preferred method of recording and, using the techniques outlined above, you should not hesitate to go on to build up a number of Tracks and Parts to make up an entire arrangement.

Figure 1.6 The recording process

Saving and opening details

Cubase provides several ways of saving material to disk and these should be fully understood before embarking on any serious projects. Files are handled using the options in the File menu. The type of file to be saved (or opened) can be recognised by its file extension and the following possibilities are available:

- .ALL. This is the file extension for a Song file. This file type includes all the arrangements currently in memory and the entire setup of Cubase, including most of the menu, dialogue box and editor settings and the drum map. This is like taking a snapshot of the current contents of the entire system.
- .ARR. This is the file extension for an Arrangement. This includes the contents of the active Arrange window, the current tempo and the Mastertrack settings. An Arrangement file is all that is needed to save the actual music itself, (when the settings of the rest of the system are not important), and it has the advantage of taking up less disk space.
- .PRT. This is the file extension for a Parts file, containing individual Parts, several Parts or Tracks. When saving, the required Part(s) must be selected or, if no Parts are selected, all Parts in the current Track will be saved. Loading a Part will input the data into the current Arrangement beginning at the left locator position and onto the same Tracks as those from which it was saved.
- .MID. This is the file extension for a MIDI file. A MIDI file is a special file format designed to allow the transfer of music between different makes of MIDI sequencer and, sometimes, between different platforms, (depending on compatibility). MIDI files usually come in two

✦ **TIP** ✦

Type O files always contain only one track which plays back on many MIDI Channels. Type 1 files contain the original track structure of the material and will include two or more tracks on separate MIDI Channels. Cubase recognises both formats and normally saves as Type 1 unless only one track is present (or all but one are muted), in which case it is saved as Type O.

formats: Type O and Type 1. MIDI files imported into Cubase may be loaded into a new Arrange window or merged into the current Arrangement at the left locator position. The Atari/Falcon version of Cubase manages MIDI files from the main open and save options of the File menu. The Mac and PC versions handle MIDI files with the import and Export options.

- .DRM. This is the file extension for Drum Maps (see the Drum edit section in Chapter 2).
- .SET. This is the file extension for a Setup file. A setup contains all the important settings of the program other than the music itself. This is useful for loading different system configurations without affecting the music currently in memory.

Part processing

Once any recording has been completed and further Tracks have been added, the role of the Arrange window starts to become more obvious. By sizing the window, even the most complicated arrangement may be viewed as a single entity and the overall structure becomes easier to see. And, of course, the opportunity to restructure the music by zooming in and manipulating specific Parts is invaluable. Manipulating Parts is one of the major functions of the Arrange window. Check out the table.

Part processing

Tool	Key held	Mouse action	Result
Pointer	–	double click between locators	creates a new Part
	–	click on Part	selects Part
	–	click/hold in white space and drag	opens stretchable grab box
	–	click/hold on Part(s) and drag	moves Part(s)
	Alt	click/hold on Part(s) and drag	copies Part(s)
	Ctrl	click/hold on Part(s) and drag	creates ghost Part(s)
Eraser	–	click on Part(s)	erases Part(s)
	–	click/hold and drag over Parts	erases Part(s)
Scissors	–	click on Part	splits Part at mouse position
	Alt	click on Part	splits Part into several smaller Parts
Magnifier	–	click/hold and drag over Part	plays Part's contents
Pencil	–	click in white space and drag	creates a new Part
	–	click/hold on end point and drag left	shortens Part
	–	click/hold on end point and drag right	lengthens Part
	Alt	click/hold on end point and drag	repeats Part over distance dragged
Mute	–	click on Part	mutes the Part
Glue	–	click on Part	joins selected Part to the next Part
	Alt	click on Part	joins Part to all following Parts

Be sure to become familiar with the manipulation of Parts using the tool-box, practising all the moves in the table on empty Parts. The ability to use the toolbox is among the most important skills in the confident handling of Cubase. Figure 1.7 clarifies the essentials of basic Part manipulation.

Figure 1.7 Basic Part manipulation

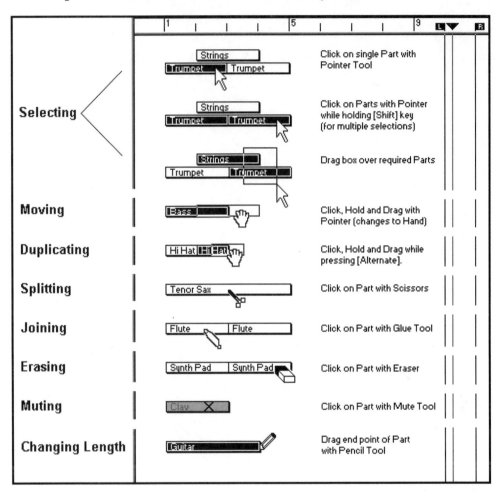

Progress report

So, what have we achieved thus far ? Well, not an awful lot musically, but then that was not the point of Chapter 1. Here we have simply armed ourselves with some of the essential tools and commands with which we can go on to more musically meaningful pursuits.

Looking back at Figure 1.1 also reveals that we have not travelled very far within the Cubase Universe. In fact, we have only just scratched the surface. This is not a problem since the idea was to give you a global per-spective before plunging more deeply. It has been rather like looking at a road map before embarking on a journey. There are no short cuts; the potential user must take things one step at a time and, as with all complex software, there will be a learning curve of some weeks before the package can be handled to a reasonable proficiency. Patience is the name of the game.

In Chapter 2 we venture out from the Arrange window to the worlds of Key, List and Drum edit.

2 ♥

Key, List and Drum edit

In Chapter 1 we looked at Cubase from a global perspective and also explored the Arrange window. This will have given the user the basic ability to record and manipulate data. We will now learn how to view and manipulate this data in fine detail in the Key, List and Drum editors.

Key edit

The recording of a Part in the Arrange window is among the first steps in getting to know Cubase. Following on from this, a large number of editing functions could be carried out on the Part. However, its contents could never actually be looked at and edited in fine detail while still remaining in the Arrange window. To look inside a Part we must go into one of the main editors.

Let's start with Key edit (Figure 2.1). To go into the editor from the Arrange window simply select Key edit from the Edit menu, or select ctrl + E on the computer keyboard. If one or more Parts are selected then this is what will be available for editing, or if no Parts are selected then all Parts in the current Track will be available for editing. Parts from up to 31 different Tracks may be selected, but most of the time you will edit single Parts.

Figure 2.1. Key edit

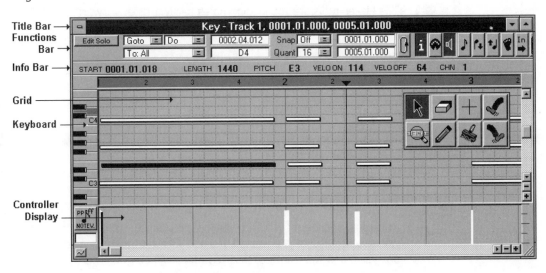

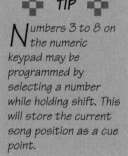

Before leaving the Arrange window it is a good idea to use alt + ctrl + P on the selected Part to set the left and right locators to its start and end points (alt + P on the Atari/Falcon version). Then select Cycle on the Transport bar, (the divide key / on the numeric keypad). Cubase will now cycle continuously on the selected Part (between the left and right locators) and, after going into Key edit, the song position can be managed with the various numeric keypad cue points such as 1, to go to the left locator, or 2, to go to the right locator etc.

Key edit appears on the screen with a grid, where the horizontal axis represents time and the vertical axis represents pitch displayed as a piano keyboard. Directly above the grid there is a position bar, showing the numbered bars and beats, and below the grid there is the controller display, where various non-note events, such as Pitch Bend and Modulation, may be displayed.

Key edit has a toolbox similar to the Arrange window but featuring four new tools for specific use in the editor. The toolbox is opened by clicking on the grid with the right mouse button and features the following.

Pointer
Similar to the Arrange window, the pointer is a general purpose tool but, this time, for selecting, moving and copying notes and events.

Eraser
The eraser is for deleting by clicking on single events or dragging over several while holding the left mouse button.

Line tool (compasses)
The line tool (Mac/PC versions) or compasses (Atari/Falcon versions) are for changing values, (usually controller data), according to a straight line drawn in the Controller display.

Kicker
The kicker tools are for jogging notes backwards or forwards by clicking on each. Notes will be moved according to the current Snap box value.

Magnifying glass
The magnifying glass is for monitoring notes by clicking on single events or dragging over several while holding the left mouse button.

Pencil tool
The pencil tool is for inserting notes, changing their lengths and for changing the values of controller events.

Brush
The brush is for pasting notes onto the grid.

Notes inserted or moved with the pointer, pencil, kicker or brush tools will be shifted onto the nearest fraction of a beat according to the Snap box value and the length of inserted notes will be governed by the Quant (quantize) box value. For insertion purposes, regard Snap as the *position* and Quant as the *length*.

Notes are displayed as graphic strips on the grid. Once a note has been selected, by clicking on it with the pointer tool (the note will turn black), its characteristics can be seen on the information bar. These include the start time, length, pitch, velocity on and off, and the channel. The info bar can be hidden or shown using the 'i' or Info button on the Functions bar of the window. Similarly, the Controller display can be hidden or shown using the control button or the small icon in the bottom left of the window in the PC versions.

There are several other icons in the Functions bar governing the set up of a loop, the reception of MIDI data and the recording of data in step-time. In addition, there are three local menus : Goto, for moving the song position pointer to various points in the Track or Part, the Select menu, dictating which data will be targeted by any chosen functions, and a useful local Do/Functions menu containing items specific to Key edit.

A further display box above the menus shows the current mouse position when it is moved into the grid area. Clicking in this box with the left mouse button changes the position display to SMPTE/time code.

But how do we put all these very obviously powerful Key edit features to good use ? Let's look at some examples from a typical Cubase session.

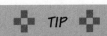

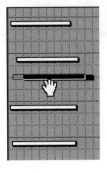
Editing a bass line

You have just recorded a perfect bass line with a great feel but some notes are too long and some overlap. Key edit is the perfect facility to remedy the situation. Proceed as follows:

- Select the pencil tool from the pop-up toolbox.
- Click and hold near the end of each offending note and drag the length back to the desired shorter duration.
- The new length can be graphically monitored on the grid and will be set to the nearest snap value as set in the Snap box. Setting this value to Off allows the maximum subtlety of length change since the pencil may be dragged in ticks (the smallest units of time or resolution measured by Cubase).

Editing note entry times

The note entry time of the chords you just played are jumbled and misplaced. The simple answer is found in Key edit as follows:

- Click and hold on the misplaced note using the pointer tool. The pointer will change to a hand.
- The whole note can now be dragged to a new position.
- For this kind of operation the snap value could once again be set to Off to facilitate the placing of notes with maximum subtlety on the grid.
- If very subtle changes in position are required, try clicking on the notes with the kicker tools to shift the start time backwards or forwards one tick at a time.

Editing timing values

The repeated melody on one of your Tracks is perfect on the first and fourth bars but out of time in bars two and three. One answer is to go into Key edit and repair the four bar Part using a stretch box and drag process. Proceed as follows:

- Set Key edit to an appropriate size to see all four bars.
- With the pointer tool selected, click and drag the mouse in empty space on the grid.
- A box will appear which can be sized around the appropriate group of notes in bars 2 and 3. The notes within the box will turn black when the mouse is released.
- Delete these notes using the 'delete' key on the computer keyboard or 'Delete events' from the Do/Functions menu.
- Select the appropriate group of notes from the first bar which will once again turn black. Select and hold any one of the blacked notes while pressing alt on the computer keyboard. A box will re-appear.
- Without releasing the mouse, drag this box, and the resulting copy of all the notes within it, to the appropriate position in the second bar. Remember that the notes will be dropped onto the nearest fraction of a beat according to the current Snap setting.
- The same procedure can then be applied to copy the repeated melody into the third bar.

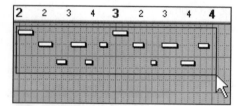 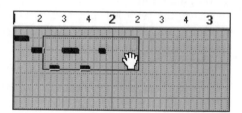

Editing note velocities

The synthesizer sound you are using produces an unwanted percussive attack on certain notes which were played with a higher velocity. To correct the situation proceed as follows:

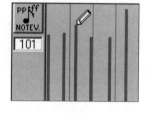

- Open Key edit and select Velocity in the Controller display by clicking on the Controller icon to the left of the display.
- The velocities of all notes should now be visible in the display as vertical strips.
- The offending velocities can be singled out and adjusted using the pencil tool.

Producing crescendos

Following on from the last example, if any crescendos (or decrescendos (diminuendos)) are required after the notes have been recorded then the controller display of Key edit is one of the best places to create them.

- Select Velocity in the Controller display.
- Click and drag using the line tool to draw in a straight line at the desired angle.

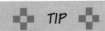

- When the mouse is released a Velocity ramp matching the straight line appears.
- This technique could be used for similar operations on other controller data such as, for example, volume events.

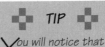

TIP

To write new events into the Controller display for any chosen controller, select the pencil tool and click, hold and drag in the display while holding 'alt'. Events will be inserted at the resolution set in the Snap box.

That's a start in using some of the principal techniques of Key edit. As a general guide to moving around among the note data on the grid you may find the following tips useful:

- Once one note has been selected, try using the left and right arrow keys to scroll through consecutive notes. This is often easier than using the mouse.
- It is also useful to actually hear each event as it is selected and this can be achieved by selecting the MIDI monitor icon (loudspeaker or ear symbol) in the top right icon panel.
- Also useful is the MIDI In icon (5 pin DIN symbol), which, along with the Note and the Velocity On and Off icons, allows the user to target data for updating via MIDI. For example, if the MIDI In and Velocity On buttons are selected you can change the Velocity On value of the currently selected note simply by playing any note on the master keyboard. Once updated, Cubase will automatically move on to the next note which can, in turn, be updated in the same manner.
- Another useful feature of Key edit is the ability to view data as it is being quantized. This provides excellent visual feedback of how the notes are actually being shifted in time.

TIP

You will notice that many mouse/keyboard combinations exhibit the same behaviour in all the main windows. In other words, selecting and dragging will simply move the event(s) or part(s) and holding alt while selecting and dragging will copy them.

Remember that any changes made in Key, or any other editor, need not be kept. Leaving Key edit using the escape key, (or clicking on 'cancel'), will return the Part back to the state it was in before you entered the editor. Leaving Key edit using 'return', (or clicking on 'keep'), will keep all changes.

List edit

And now let's move on to List edit. List edit (Figure 2.2) differs from the other editors in that all kinds of MIDI data and special Cubase events may be accessed and updated, including System Exclusive.

Open List edit using the Edit menu or select ctrl + G on the computer keyboard. Similar to Key edit, List edit features a grid, but of far greater importance and far more useful are the columns hidden behind the grid which can be revealed by moving the split point to the right of the screen. The columns contain information about each MIDI event including its start

TIP

The general handling of Key, List and Drum edit are very similar and many of the important editing commands outlined above are common to all three.

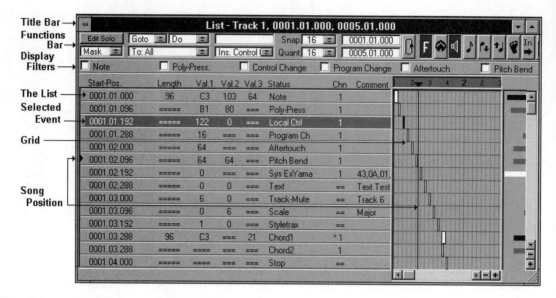

Figure 2.2 List edit

position, length, status and MIDI channel. There are also the value columns, (Val 1, Val 2 and Val 3), which will be active or not active according to the event type.

For example, ordinary note events will feature their pitch in the value 1 column followed by their Velocity On and Off values in the value 2 and value 3 columns, but a controller event will be active in the value 1 and value 2 columns only. Many events will have no entry in the Comment column. However, the Comment column for a System Exclusive event will contain the System Exclusive message itself.

Functions which are unique to List edit include the Mask menu, the Insert bar (Ins), and the Display filters. These are found in the Functions bar above the list.

- The Mask menu may be used to force a display of all data of the same event type as the currently selected event or of all data with the same event type and the same values as the currently selected event. All other events will be hidden from view.
- The Insert bar contains a pop-up menu for the selection of event types. Any chosen type of data may be inserted into the list by clicking with the pencil tool on the grid.
- In the Atari/Falcon version, the Display filters are comprised of six boxes containing letters representing different event types. NO is for note, PP is for polyphonic pressure, CT is for controller, PC is for program change, AT is for aftertouch and PB is for pitch bend. When the letters are in upper-case the event type is displayed in the Event list but, if you click on the box, the letters change to lower-case and the event type is not displayed. In the Mac and PC versions, the event types are displayed or filtered according to tick boxes which are opened using the Function bar's 'F' button. With the Display filters, users can target certain types of data by hiding the rest.

The Display filters and the Mask functions are among the most useful features of List edit but they should not be confused. The Display filters hide the chosen data from view but, unlike Mask, they do not hide the data from editing. With the filters any global editing operation will still affect all events regardless of what is currently displayed. Mask, however, completely shields the hidden data from any editing operation.

In List edit, the events themselves may be edited by clicking and holding in the columns with the left or right mouse button on any of the changeable values of the chosen event. For example, it is a simple matter to change the velocity of a note by clicking and holding in the value 2 column of the chosen event. The right mouse button will increase the value and the left mouse button will decrease it. All values in the columns are changeable using the mouse buttons but it is not possible to change the events from one type to another in the status column. Remember also the graphic display to the right of the grid. When the mouse pointer is moved into this area it is automatically changed to a pencil tool. The horizontal bars in the display represent the velocities of notes or the Val 2 values of most other MIDI event types. Here, events may be changed in much the same way as in the Controller display of Key edit.

As we can see, there is one essential difference between List and Key edit. Whereas Key edit is directed towards the graphic editing of note data on the grid and controller data in the Controller display, List edit is directed towards the somewhat more detailed editing of any type of MIDI event and its various values in the display list. So, as a general rule, List edit is probably most useful for the editing of non-note events, and, (particularly with the addition of the SysEx editor Module in the Atari/Falcon Score version), it is an essential tool for viewing and changing SysEx data. And there are, of course, those types of data which cannot be viewed and edited anywhere else, such as track mute, text and MIDI mixer events. But let's look at some specific examples which may prove useful to a number of users.

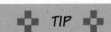

Editing System Exclusive messages

For the editing of System Exclusive messages proceed as follows:

- Select the SysEx event, (which will appear in the list and on the grid as a single block), and click once in the Comment column.
- The message itself will then appear in a pop-up box on screen as Hexadecimal code.
- Edit the message as desired and press return to keep the data.

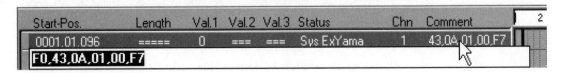

The Atari/Falcon version's SysEx editor module allows access to longer messages. However, a good knowledge of System Exclusive is required to make any meaningful changes.

Finding unwanted program change messages

At some time in their lives most Cubase users will suffer from the problem of an unwanted or incorrect program change (or some other data such as a volume controller) embedded somewhere among the rest of the data. This is not always easy to find for deletion or editing. With the List edit filters the task is easy.

- Click on or tick the filter boxes of all those event types you do *not* wish to see.
- The unwanted event(s) can now be found more easily among the remaining unfiltered data displayed in the list.

☑ Note		☑ Poly-Press.			☑ Control Change		☐ Program Change			
Start-Pos.	Length	Val.1	Val.2	Val.3	Status		2	3	4	2
0001.01.000	=====	2	===	===	Program Ch					
0002.01.000	=====	12	===	===	Program Ch					

Inserting a Local Off controller event

Most users will have their master keyboard set to Local Off for use with Cubase. One problem is that some synthesizers used as master keyboards power up with Local On. This means that the user must manually set the keyboard to Local Off at the start of each session. However, using List edit, a Local Off controller event may be inserted into a Part. This could be included in the DEF file which is first loaded into Cubase when the system is booted up. To insert the appropriate event, proceed as follows:

- Select Controller in the 'Ins' box.
- Select the pencil tool in the grid and click with the left mouse (at the beginning of the Part, for example). A new controller event with various default values will be inserted into the list.
- Click and hold in the value 1 column to change the controller number to 122, the Local On/Off controller.
- Set the controller to 0 in the value 2 column, which is the Off setting (the On setting would have been 127).

Start-Pos.	Length	Val.1	Val.2	Val.3	Status		2	3	4	2
0001.02.000	=====	122	0	===	Local Ctrl					

When the Part is played the target keyboard will be set to Local Off. This is assuming that the keyboard responds to this controller. Most modern synths do. This technique could be used for the input of similar controllers or any other event types.

Changing all settings to same value

Sometimes it is appropriate to change all the settings in one column of List edit to the same value.

- Hold 'alt' while clicking and holding with the left or right mouse buttons on any value in the chosen column.
- Increase or decrease the value appropriately and when the mouse button is released, all values in that column (for the same event types) will change to the same setting simultaneously.

Start-Pos.	Length	Val.1	Val.2	Val.3	Status
0003.01.297	202	F#4	75	0	Note
0003.02.190	125	E4	75	0	Note
0003.03.001	274	F#4	75	0	Note
0003.03.295	241	E4	75	0	Note
0003.04.193	188	F#4	75	0	Note

Other aspects of List edit worth considering include the following:

- A further column may be added to List edit by clicking in the mouse position indicator bar. This will change the position display to SMPTE/EBU time and the list will now feature two columns showing the Time code start and end points for each event. In fact, the Time code end column replaces the Length column. This is useful for circumstances when the precise timing of events is crucial.
- Remember that quantize works on notes alone, so other kinds of events will remain at their original positions.
- Unlike Key edit, only one Track or selected Parts from one Track, may be edited in List edit at any one time.

Drum edit

And now let's move onto the third of Cubase's main editors, Drum edit (Figure 2.3). As the name implies, this is designed for the editing of drum or percussion data. You should be aware , however, that it is not absolutely essential to view this kind of data in Drum edit. It could equally be viewed in any of the other editors. However, if a MIDI Track is converted into a Drum Track the data will be adapted for specific uses in Drum edit. This will become clearer as we go on.

Drum edit features a grid with time on the horizontal axis and the drum or percussion instruments on the vertical axis. Pulling the split point to the right reveals a number of columns, most of which are unique to Drum edit.

If the Track to be edited is classed as a Drum Track, the columns will feature the following : the Mute column (M), for the muting of individual drum instruments, the Sound column, for naming each drum sound, the Quantize column (Quant), where each sound may have an individual quantize value, the Input note column (I-Note), defining the note value controlling each sound, the Output note column (O-Note), defining the target note departing from the MIDI Out of Cubase, the Length column (Len), defining a fixed length for each sound, the Channel column (Chn), for the

Title Bar
Functions
Bar
Info Bar
Grid
Drum Map
Controller
Display

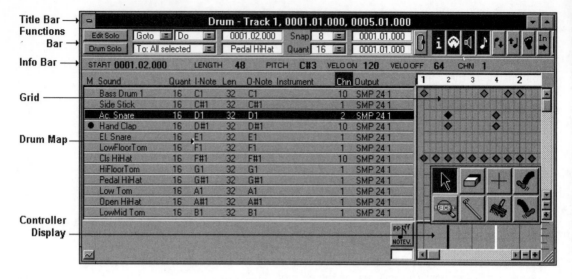

Figure 2.3 Drum edit

selection of a MIDI channel for each sound, the Output column, for the selection of the MIDI device output for each sound, the Instrument column, for the naming of combinations of the Channel and Output columns, and the four level columns, where four preset velocity levels may be set for each sound when events are inserted using the mouse on the grid or in step time. If the Track to be edited is a MIDI track, the output note (O-Note), Instrument and Output columns are omitted.

Using the grid is similar to the other editors. However, knowing how to manage the columns is probably the most important requirement for using Drum edit successfully.

Set up the Drum Map

Before recording any drum data it is a good idea to have first set up the Drum Map. The Drum Map is simply a set of 64 drum sound names each with their corresponding values in the columns. It is not possible to have more than one Drum Map in Cubase at the same time. Here we will be considering the procedure for a Drum Track. This shows Drum edit in its most adaptable mode. Proceed as follows:

- Create an empty Part on a Track on the Arrange window and change the Track class to Drum Track. A small drumstick symbol will appear in the class column.
- Go into Drum edit by selecting from the edit menu or using ctrl+D on the computer keyboard.
- Let's update the I-Note (input note) and O-Note (output note) columns to the desired settings via MIDI, followed by entering the appropriate names in the Sound column. Ensure that the master keyboard is playing the target drum or percussion sounds through Cubase. These could be, for example, the sounds of a drum machine.
- Select the MIDI In icon from the Functions bar in the top right of the window.

- Go to the first sound in the sound list by clicking on it once with the left mouse and then select the I-Note column.
- Play the first sound on the keyboard and this note value will be automatically entered into the I-Note column for the currently selected sound.
- Press the down arrow on the computer keyboard to go to the next sound.
- Enter the next note via MIDI and proceed similarly until all sounds have been entered.
- Follow exactly the same procedure for the O-Note column so that the input and output notes match. (Remember that, for more complicated Drum Maps, the input and output notes need not match at all. This is explained in more detail below).
- Double click on each sound and enter an appropriate name into the pop-up box.
- The Channel column could also be changed accordingly if sounds are being targeted on more than one MIDI channel. However, for multi channel operation, 'Any' must be selected in the Track's channel column on the Arrange window.

TIP

For multi MIDI channel operation from Drum edit, 'Any' must be selected in the Drum Track's Channel column in the Arrange window

So what is the point of having an I-Note (input) and an O-Note (output) column in Drum edit ? The idea is to facilitate the user's quick selection of drum and percussion sources while maintaining the kit in a standard position on the keyboard. In other words, if you are used to having the bass drum on C1 (36), but the bass drum in the target unit is on C2 (48), then you could set the I-Note column to C1 (36) and the O-Note column to D2 (48). It makes things clearer to view the I-Note column as a representation of where the sounds are being played on the keyboard and the O-Note column as a representation of where the sounds are found in the target unit.

The note positions in the O-Note column could be literally anywhere in the MIDI range and, by keeping the I-Note column notes static, we have avoided some of the complex mapping and transposition problems which are often associated with building a MIDI kit.

For example, imagine the current Drum Map is set to play a Roland TR808 drum machine but later it is decided that a replacement sound for the snare is required using a sampled sound from an Akai S1000. All that is needed is to change the appropriate snare sound O-Note column to the position of the replacement sound and the MIDI channel column to that of the S1000. Any music already programmed will be playing the new sound immediately. No more awkward re-arranging and transposition. The procedure is also excellent for quickly seeking and trying out alternative sounds for any drum or percussion set up. As time goes on users will establish a number of Drum Maps which relate specifically to the units in their set-up.

Drum Maps can be saved or loaded from the File menu using the Drum Map file type. All Drum Map files are given the file extension .DRM.

And now let's clarify the use of some of the other Drum edit features:

- The Length and Quant (quantize) columns and level 1 to 4 columns apply when inserting events graphically on the grid or inputting notes in step time.
- Inserting will involve the use of the toolbox. You may have already noticed that Drum edit's toolbox differs slightly from the other editors in that the pencil tool has been replaced by a drumstick tool.

- The drumstick differs in that it cannot be held and dragged on the grid to adjust the length of a note as it is being inserted. Each Drum edit event's length is governed by the duration set in the Length column. However, if you click, hold and drag the drumstick horizontally along the grid, for one sound, events will be written in at the resolution set by the quantize column for that sound. This could be useful for quickly writing in some closed hi-hats at 1/16 note intervals. In addition, if clicked over an already existing event, the drumstick will delete that event.
- When inserting notes with the drumstick their velocity level can be managed using the level 1 to 4 columns. Each of the level columns can be separately adjusted for each sound and the choice of level is selected by holding various keys on the computer keyboard. Holding no key when inserting an event selects Level 1, holding 'shift' selects level 2, holding 'ctrl' selects level 3 and holding 'ctrl + shift' selects level 4.
- Similar to Key edit, Drum edit features an Info line, where existing events can be updated in terms of their note value, velocity and length etc.
- Drum edit also has a Controller display but it differs from Key edit in that it shows exclusively the controller data for the currently selected sound.
- Also new is the Solo button which, as expected, mutes all sounds other than the currently selected one. Other mute configurations can be set up by clicking directly in the Mute column.

Smart moves

That's it for Chapter 2. It's now up to you to experiment until the main editing moves become second nature. To this end the table shows some principal mouse and keyboard moves which are useable in all three editors.

Remember that as well as going from the Arrange window to any editor, you can also go directly from one editor to another, which is often extremely useful for detailed work. In addition, by holding shift while opening each editor (alt on the Atari/Falcon version), several editors may be opened at the same time and tiled onto the screen, using File in the Windows menu.

Smart moves

Tool	Key held	Mouse action	Result
Pointer	–	click on event	selects event
	–	click/hold on event and drag	moves event
	alt	click/hold on event and drag	copies event
	–	click/hold and drag on grid	opens stretchable grab box
	–	click/hold on value with left mouse	decreases value
	–	click/hold on value with right mouse	increases value
	shift	click/hold on value with left mouse	decreases value in tens
	shift	click/hold on value with right mouse	increases value in tens
	–	double click on value	opens pop-up input box
Eraser	–	click on event	deletes event
Line tool	–	click and drag in Controller display	changes values in straight lines
Magnifier	–	click on note	monitors selected note
Pencil	–	click/hold on event and drag	changes length of event
	–	click on grid	inputs an event
	–	click on events in Controller display	changes values of events
	alt	click and drag in Controller display	inserts new controller events
Paintbrush	–	click/hold and drag	paints in events on one pitch
	alt	click/hold and drag	paints in events anywhere on grid
–	return	–	keeps edits
–	esc	–	discards edits

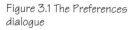

3

More editing and control functions

Chapters 1 and 2 have explored some of the major working areas of Cubase. However, the system is also packed full of smaller but equally useful features which help in the routine manipulation and control of MIDI data. Most of these features are found in the main menus.

System preparation

Let's start with three menu items which are concerned with the general setting up and handling of the system: Preferences, MIDI Setup and MIDI Filter. Some readers may be thinking that these features should have been dealt with at the very beginning, but you cannot effectively update a system to your own settings if you do not first understand that system's structure.

Normally Cubase is supplied with its important features already sensibly set in the Definition files. However, users, now more familiar with the program, will almost certainly wish to enter their own custom settings which can then be saved as a new 'DEF.ALL' file.

Preferences

Selecting Preferences in the File menu opens a dialogue box (Figure 3.1) where the user may select:

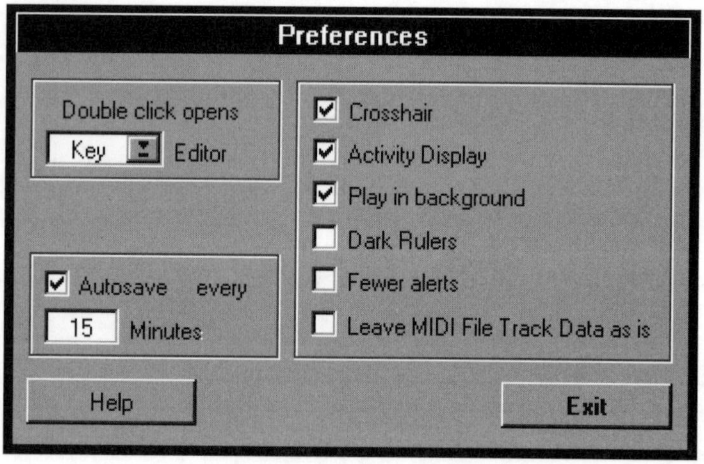

Figure 3.1 The Preferences dialogue

- 'Double click opens', to select the choice of editor (Key, List or Score), when the user double clicks on a Part.
- 'Autosave', to automatically save the current song as backup.all at the time interval shown in the minutes box. This provides a safety copy which can be indispensable in the event of a system crash.
- 'Crosshair cursor', to show a crosshair comprising of a dynamic cross of vertical and horizontal lines which indicates the precise mouse position on the Arrange window grid. This is useful for the accurate positioning of Parts.
- 'Activity display', to show the Activity column in the Arrange window.
- play in background, to allow Cubase to play in the background behind another launched program.
- 'Dark rulers', to darken the appearance of the position bar in the Arrange window and editors.
- 'Fewer alerts', to disable the pop-up warning dialogues which appear for various editing operations. For expert users only.
- 'Leave MIDI File Track data as is', to leave imported MIDI files exactly as they are found on disk , (when ticked), or to separate the data out onto individual tracks (unticked). Most users should leave this option unticked.

The Atari/Falcon version contains a different set of preferences with the following replacing some of the above options:

- 'Increase by left mouse', to increase values with the left mouse button rather than the default right mouse.
- 'Real-time scroll', to switch on or off the real-time scroll of the windows as the music is played.
- 'Do-re-mi text', to name note values as do, re, mi etc. instead of the usual letters.
- 'Background follow', to follow the song in any window even if it is not the active window.

Different options are available depending on which version of Cubase is being used.

MIDI Setup

MIDI Setup is found in the Options menu (Figure 3.2). This is where users set up various global parameters which govern the manner in which Cubase handles MIDI. MIDI Thru is among the most important and, in most cases, this would be set to active so that incoming MIDI data is echoed to the MIDI Out.

But why is it necessary to have the MIDI Thru activated in the first place ? The answer is that to communicate with the MIDI units in the system the data from the master keyboard must travel *through* Cubase to reach them. When the MIDI Thru is de-activated the data stops inside Cubase. With the Thru function activated, the data arriving at the MIDI In is echoed to the MIDI Out, and the user may play any unit in the system

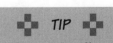
TIP

*C**ubase also offers the possibility to switch the Thru off for one unique MIDI channel (for those users with a master keyboard not equipped with a Local Off function).*

Figure 3.2 The MIDI setup
dialogue

Figure 3.2 The MIDI setup
dialogue

simply by changing the MIDI channel of the currently selected Track in the
Arrange window. To avoid double sounding notes and other complications
when playing the master keyboard, it is advisable to switch it to local off
mode. This cuts the physical keyboard feed to the synthesis part of the
instrument such that it will only play from the data received at its MIDI In
via Cubase (see Figure 1.5 in Chapter 1).

MIDI setup also allows the user to re-map any one controller to any
other. For example, a Pan controller (controller 10) could be under the
command of the master keyboard's modulation wheel (controller 1) by
mapping Modulation to Pan in the Controller section of the setup window.

Running status is a MIDI data compression technique in the MIDI protocol which is sent out from Cubase by default. Sometimes this causes
problems with older synthesizers and this part of the window gives the
user the opportunity to de-activate it for any of the output ports.

MIDI setup's global parameters section contains a number of miscellaneous features which affect the handling of various details of the software:

- 'Groups take Part mute' toggles the ability to mute or not mute the
  Parts in a group from the mute columns of the original Tracks.
- 'Note off' toggles between sending real Note Off messages (ticked) and
  Note Off messages as Note On with zero velocity (unticked).
- 'Activating reset on track change' sends out a reset of pitch bend,
  modulation and channel pressure when changing Tracks.
- 'Activating reset on Part end' sends out a reset of pitch bend,
  modulation, sustain pedal and channel pressure when each Part comes
  to an end.
- 'Activating reset on stop' sends out a reset of pitch bend, modulation
  and channel pressure for all Tracks plus All Notes Off and Reset All
  Controllers messages when Cubase is stopped. The reset options avoid
  such things as hanging notes and hanging pitch bends.
- 'Activating Note On priority' ensures that Note On messages are always
  given timing priority over all other message types, resulting in a tighter

mix during passages containing a heavy output of controller and other non-note messages.

- 'Length correction' attempts to ensure that there is always at least a short amount of time (measured in ticks) between a Note Off and Note On message on the same pitch and MIDI channel in order to avoid lost notes.
- 'Play parameter delay' allows the user to anticipate or delay the time (in ticks) at which the play parameters of the Inspector are sent out. Most often it will be set to a negative value in order to allow the target synth time to react to such things as bank or program changes.

Remember that MIDI setup comes preset to sensible settings in the definition files supplied with the program but you may now wish to experiment with your own settings.

MIDI Filter

MIDI Filter, also found in the Options menu (Figure 3.3), is used to filter out unwanted MIDI data. The dialogue box allows the main types of MIDI data to be filtered from the record and thru paths of Cubase, and it allows the filtering of one or more MIDI channels and up to four different types of continuous controllers for data arriving at the MIDI input.

Figure 3.3 The MIDI Filter dialogue

The following flow chart should clarify matters:

Figure 3.4 MIDI Filter
flowchart

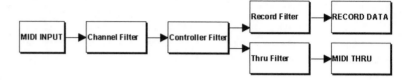

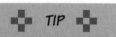
Filtering data during recording is particularly useful when, for example, the master keyboard is outputting unwanted aftertouch data, (especially if the target synth does not even respond to this kind of data). System Exclusive data may be equally unwanted. In fact, most users leave SysEx and aftertouch filtered as the default setting and only allow this kind of data into the system when it is specifically desired. You could equally filter SysEx and aftertouch from the Thru section.

Whereas the record and thru filters provide for the blanket removal of all controller data from the incoming MIDI messages, the controller filter may be set to remove up to four specific continuous controllers. For example, this could be useful for discarding all modulation data but keeping all other controller data contained within the incoming MIDI messages. When required, each controller filter may be de-activated by setting it to 'no ctrl'.

The channel filter might be useful for transferring an arrangement from an external sequencer into Cubase when, for example, only the drums on MIDI channel 10 were required. All other channels could be filtered and the drums alone would be transferred.

Cubase in colour

Further visual customisation of Cubase is possible when running the Mac and PC versions in colour. On the PC try changing the background of the Arrange window using Part background in the Options menu. From here it is possible to load any Windows Bitmap to appear as the background of the Part display. Several choices are supplied with the program and are found in the textures folder. However, if you require a simpler visual background, such as plain white or grey, you might like to create your own bitmaps in a windows image editing program like Paintbrush. Simply load in an existing small sized bitmap file and paint it the colour required. Re-save as a bitmap under a new name and load it as the part background, as described above.

As for the Parts themselves, seven user definable colours are available using the Part colors pop-up on the Arrange window status bar. Simply select a Track or Part(s) and choose a colour from the menu.

Colour is also available in the editors by clicking on the colour palette icon found on the extreme right of the Functions bar. Events may be all white, or colour coded according to their channel, pitch, velocity or which Part they belong to. The chosen colours for channel, pitch and velocity may be customised using the edit ... colours option. The use of colour in the editors is excellent for clarifying the status of events and, in the case of velocity colours, provides a clearer impression of the velocity of the notes without necessarily showing velocity in the controller display.

Structural editing actions

Cut, copy and paste

Cut, copy and paste will already be familiar to readers who have used a word processor. These functions are found in the edit menu but may also be selected using the standard ctrl + X for cut, ctrl + C for copy and ctrl + V for paste. Similar to a word processor, the chosen cut or copied data is stored in a temporary, invisible clipboard, ready to be pasted to a new location.

In the Arrange window, Parts or whole arrangements may be cut or copied into the clipboard by simply selecting the Parts required and then choosing cut or copy from the Edit menu or from the computer keyboard. The chosen data may be pasted back into the same Arrange window at a new position, according to the song position pointer, or into a different Arrange window where new Tracks will be automatically created for the pasted Parts. Data may be pasted from the clipboard as many times as required since it is *copied* from the clipboard, not *moved* from it. Groups of notes and other kinds of MIDI data can be similarly manipulated in the edit windows. Note, however, that data may be selected from a number of different Parts but it is always pasted into the *active* part at the song position pointer.

Cut, copy and paste are best for moving or copying data to positions many bars later in the song, for managing large amounts of data or for copying between separate arrangements.

Repeat

Also in the realms of moving data around, you should not forget 'Repeat', found in the Structure menu or selected with ctrl + K, for the repeating of a single Part or a group of Parts in the Arrange window. This opens a small dialogue box where you may select the number of copies required and choose whether the copied Parts are to be ghost or real. The resulting copies will be automatically pasted onto the display, immediately after the original.

Repeat is the best option whenever Parts need to be repeated several times in a row and it has the added advantage of saving on memory when ghost copies are chosen.

Global concerns

For the bulk manipulation of data in the Arrange window try Global cut, Global insert and Global split. Global cut and Global insert are best explained in terms of viewing the Arrange window as a length of recording tape.

- Using the left and right locators to mark the positions of the appropriate section of music, Global cut will simply completely remove all data on all Tracks between these points and join the remaining music together where the section has been removed. It is just like removing a section of recording tape with a razor blade.
- Global Insert will simply insert a piece of virtual 'blank tape' between the locators, using the left locator position as the point from which the existing music will be shifted forward to just after the right locator.
- Global split simultaneously splits all Parts at the left and right locator positions, similar to the action of the Scissors tool used to split individual Parts.

In all three global cases, muted Tracks will not be subjected to the editing action.

The global functions provide invaluable editing power when the arrangement has become a complex affair, such as when last minute changes require the middle 8 to be a middle 16, (or vice versa), or when the Intro. needs to be four bars longer!

Remix and Mixdown

Repeat, Global cut and Global insert manipulate the data in a linear fashion but what about splitting and mixing data vertically between Tracks? Remix and Mixdown, found in the Structure menu, provide the answer for certain structural editing requirements of this kind.

Remix

Remix is used to automatically extract a number of separate Tracks, based on the MIDI channel of events, from an original multi-channel Part or Track. In other words, if an arrangement has been recorded into Cubase from an external sequencer and all the data has ended up on a single Track which has been set to 'Any', this data may be separated out onto different Tracks according to the MIDI channel of each Event. Reasons for doing this might include the need to process or edit different Parts of the arrangement separately, or to simply obtain a better overview of the actual structural content.

Before performing the Remix, ensure that the left and right locators are set to the start and end positions of the target sequence. Upon selecting Remix from the menu, all data between the locators will be copied over to separate Tracks according to their MIDI channel, new Tracks being created automatically and the MIDI channel column being automatically numbered according to the MIDI channel of each Track's contents. Remix is also useful for separating the contents of type 0 MIDI files.

Mixdown

Mixdown, also found in the Structure menu, performs the opposite function of Remix, i.e. the merging of all data on a number of Tracks into one single composite Part on a new Track. Simply set the left and right locators to the section of the song required, create a new Track and select it ready for the Mixdown Part. Then select Mixdown from the menu. All Tracks will be merged into a new composite Part, entitled 'Mixdown', and the data will assume the appropriate MIDI channel values as found in the channel column for each Track.

Any Tracks not required should simply be muted in the Mute column and they will not be included. To enable the new composite Track to play back normally, 'Any' should be selected in its channel column. Note that any of the Inspector's playback parameters, such as transposition or velocity changes, will be permanently written into the new mixdown Part.

Mixdown is useful for producing composite drum or percussion Parts, or bringing together disparate Tracks or harmony lines which are on the same MIDI channel. It can also simply help in tidying up an untidy arrangement.

The Inspector

The Inspector is found in the Arrange window to the left of the Arrange columns (Figure 3.5). It is opened and closed by clicking on the square shaped icon in the lower left corner of the screen. The Inspector contains a number of parameters, (referred to as the Playback Parameters), which can be changed to affect the playback of the currently selected Part(s) or Track. These changes are not recorded into the data in any permanent form.

Figure 3.5 The Inspector

Bank and Program Change
Most obvious are the Bank and Program Change parameters which simply change the bank or program number in the target unit. Note, however, that when the Bank select function is changed it also sends out the current program change. These functions are useful, firstly, for quickly searching for the desired patch on a synth by remote control from the comfort of the arrange screen and, secondly, for recording automatic program changes into Parts and Tracks. In addition, if the GM Module/editor is active, then sounds may be selected by name rather than number.

Volume
Volume is useful for setting up a basic mix of the current arrangement by changing the relative levels of each Part or Track.

Transpose
Transpose is useful for trying out simple harmonies or shifting the octave for any given sound.

Velocity
Velocity affects the velocity dynamics of the MIDI data, in the simple sense of adding or subtracting a value.

Delay

Delay could be used for changing the feel of the chosen Part(s) or Track in relation to the others, by shifting the data backwards or forwards in time by a number of ticks. The actual amount of time in fractions of a second will vary, depending on the current tempo. Possible uses might include adjusting a snare or hi-hat Track to be late or early to give the drum arrangement a special feel, or shifting a slow strings sound earlier to anticipate the beat and overcome the late feel of their slow attack time.

Length

Length might be used to increase the staccato feel of the Part by using a setting of 25%. To increase a Part's legato try a value of 150% or more.

Compression

Compression also affects the velocity dynamics of the MIDI data but by dividing or multiplying according to a percentage. Velocity and Compression could be used together to flatten out the dynamics of an over-excited Part (try settings of + 50 for Velocity with 50 % Compression), or to add dynamics to a static sounding part (– 30 for Velocity with 175 % Compression).

Pan

Pan is used to set up the position of each Track or Part in the stereo image and like Volume helps set up a basic mix of the arrangement.

The Inspector therefore provides an excellent facility for quickly experimenting with the data without the fear of irreversibly changing it. The immediately useful functions are shown in the table. This outlines the functions and range of each parameter, gives some example settings and shows their effect on the MIDI data.

Inspector examples

Inspector Parameter	Function	Range	Example Setting	Result
Bank	bank change	(off) 0–16383	1	sends MIDI Bank select 1
Program	program change(off)	1–128	1	sends MIDI Program change 1
Volume	volume controller (7)	(off) 0–127	100	sends MIDI Vol. controller set at 100.
Transpose	pitch change	–127 +127	–12	transposes pitch down by 1 octave
Velocity	velocity change	–127 +127	10	raises all note velocities by 10
Delay	time shift	–127 +127 ticks	–5	shifts selected part slightly ahead in time
Length	changes note duration	(off) 25% – 200%	25%	cuts length of notes to 1/4 of current length
			200%	doubles the current length
Compression	velocity compression/ expansion	(off) 25% – 200%	25%	current velocity values are divided by 4
			200%	current velocity values are doubled
Pan	pan position	(off) L63 – R63	R63	pans sound to the extreme right

Beware of using too many Playback Parameters in an arrangement since, due to the fact that the changes are processed in real-time, this could lead to an unnecessary drain on the computer's processing power. Once you are absolutely sure that the changes made in the Inspector will never be updated, use Freeze Playback Parameters in the functions menu (alt + ctrl + F) to make them a permanent part of the data.

Quantize

The quantize functions found in the Functions menu are among Cubase's most used features. These warrant detailed inspection. Far from being a mere timing correction function, with Cubase, quantize has become a creative tool in its own right.

It is apparent from the menu items that various different kinds of quantize operations are possible but the principle is the same for all of them; quantize shifts notes onto or towards the division of the bar set in the Quant (quantize) box. The rules of actually how this is done depends on the type of quantize chosen.

Over quantize
Over quantize (Q on the computer keyboard) simply shifts notes onto the nearest quantize value, but it also has the ability to detect if the playing is consistently behind or in front of the beat and it will quantize chords intelligently.

Note on quantize
Note On quantize (W on the computer keyboard), is the least musical quantize method. It uses the Note On element of notes to shift them onto the nearest quantize value with no regard for their particular context. The original note length remains unchanged.

Iterative quantize
Iterative quantize (E on the computer keyboard), takes things one stage further since the user can set up Strength and Don't Q (Don't quantize) parameters, (in the Setup/Edit Grooves dialogue), to govern the manner in which notes will be shifted *towards* the quantize value. Don't Q tells Cubase the range *close* to the quantize value, (in ticks), within which no Iterative quantize action will take place, and the Strength percentage tells Cubase how far to shift notes that are not close enough to the quantize value. Due to its progressive nature, Iterative quantize may be selected a number of times in succession.

Analytic quantize
Analytic quantize intelligently corrects timing errors according to an analysis of the music based on the quantize value and the actual characteristics of the contents. This is best suited to rhythmically complex input and solos and is worth trying if none of the other quantize methods give the desired result.

Match quantize

Match quantize is a special kind of quantize function provided in the Arrange window toolbox (Match Q). It is designed to impose the timing and accent characteristics (the feel) of one Part upon another. For example, this could be used to tighten up the feel of bass line and bass drum Parts. Use the bass drum Part as the 'feel' Part and simply drag it, using the Match Q Tool, and let go over the target bass line Part. A dialogue box will ask if the velocity values should also be matched. In this example, 'No' is probably the best option. The quantize value selected for this operation will govern the capture range.

If a coarse quantize Value has been selected, such as 4, then more data in the target Part will be dragged to the positions of the notes in the feel Part, (which, in this case, would probably not be desirable). Selecting a quantize value of 16 or 8 would ensure that the bass line remains intact, with most of the notes slipping through unchanged, and only those notes closest to those in the feel part (the bass drum) being shifted back or forth in time.

Groove quantize

Groove quantize, (J on the computer keyboard), takes Match quantize one stage further. It allows the user to store a number of Groove Maps for creating rhythmic feels. Each Groove Map is a feel template which may be imposed upon any chosen data. A selection of grooves are supplied with the program but these may be updated or completely replaced by new sets of grooves designed by the user or outside sources. Using the existing preset grooves on suitable material can produce startling results. (Pressing J on the computer keyboard repeats the most recently selected Groove).

As with most Cubase processing, the final judge of whether something is working or not is the ear, and this is certainly true of quantize. However, the maze of quantize parameters involved may obscure what is actually going on and what result is required. Visual feedback may help clarify matters and Figure 3.6 shows the results of various kinds of quantize on a very simple drum Part in Key edit.

The snare drum (D1) and the hi-hat (F#1) on the second beat of the second bar have been recorded very inaccurately and the displays show how each quantize method changes the data. The hi-hat has been recorded nearer to the third beat of the bar than the snare, and thus, for both Note On and Iterative quantize, gets pulled across to this beat rather than onto the desired second beat.

Over Quantize alone produces a satisfactory result since this method treats the snare and hi-hat events intelligently (as a kind of chord) and shifts them back to the same position. Note also that Iterative quantize has no further effect on the data after the second selection because all notes are already within the chosen 48 tick 'Don't quantize' zone. Of course, the quantizing of more sophisticated data may prove much more complicated and only experience, experimentation and understanding will help perfect the process.

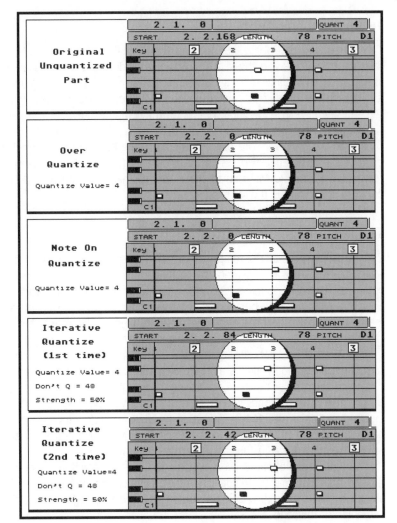

Figure 3.6 Quantize results –
Over quantize alone produces
a satisfactory result

You should be aware that quantize works on notes alone, leaving other kinds of MIDI messages unchanged. In addition, quantize does not permanently change the data, and except for Iterative quantize the original notes are always used for calculating subsequent quantize actions. Undo quantize (U on the computer keyboard) will return a quantized part to its original state. Remember also that Cubase provides quantize values of any resolution between 64th and whole notes with triplet and dotted options for each. The choice of quantize value is crucial to a successful result.

Finally Freeze quantize makes the current quantizing status permanent. This should be used to permanently lock the quantize into Parts only when it is sure they will never need re-processing.

Tempo management

The Mastertrack is Cubase's tempo and time signature manager. It is, in fact, another Track like those in the Arrange window but it is specialised in its own kind of data. It comes in graphic or list form, each of which has its own unique display. It can be opened by selecting Mastertrack from the edit menu, or by pressing ctrl + M on the computer keyboard. It contains tempo, time signature and other information.

The Mac and PC versions of Cubase feature the Mastertrack in graphic or list forms as standard parts of the program. The Atari/Falcon version features the graphic Mastertrack as a module named Cuetrax and the default Mastertrack is the list version.

The Mastertrack list editor

Cubase usually runs at the tempo set on the Transport bar, but when the Mastertrack button is activated (by clicking on it or pressing M on the computer keyboard) Cubase follows the tempo(s) set in the Mastertrack. Even if the Mastertrack button has not been activated, all time signatures in the display will be present in the Arrange window. However, tempo changes occur only when the button has been activated.

The Mastertrack list display (Figure 3.7) is managed using various commands in the local menus at the top of the window. The time signatures and tempi may be changed directly in the display by using the left and right mouse buttons. With the Atari/Falcon version, the position of inserted events is decided by adjusting the Mastertrack window's song position *before* they are added to the list. Neither the bar number nor the SMPTE position are adjustable directly in the display list.

The functioning of the PC version is easier since the positions of events may be adjusted directly in the display. Remember that the Mastertrack always contains at least one initial tempo and one time signature at the beginning of the song.

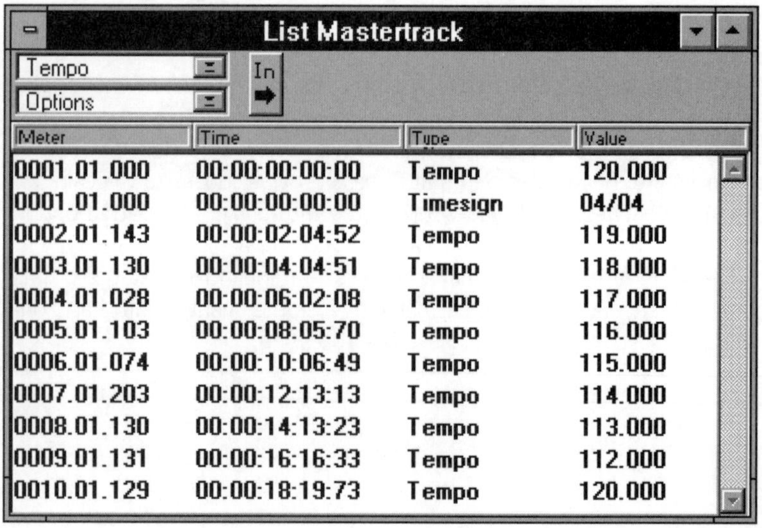

Figure 3.7 The Mastertrack list display

List Mastertrack

Tempo

Options

In

Meter	Time	Type	Value
0001.01.000	00:00:00:00:00	Tempo	120.000
0001.01.000	00:00:00:00:00	Timesign	04/04
0002.01.143	00:00:02:04:52	Tempo	119.000
0003.01.130	00:00:04:04:51	Tempo	118.000
0004.01.028	00:00:06:02:08	Tempo	117.000
0005.01.103	00:00:08:05:70	Tempo	116.000
0006.01.074	00:00:10:06:49	Tempo	115.000
0007.01.203	00:00:12:13:13	Tempo	114.000
0008.01.130	00:00:14:13:23	Tempo	113.000
0009.01.131	00:00:16:16:33	Tempo	112.000
0010.01.129	00:00:18:19:73	Tempo	120.000

Regardless of whether any tempo changes are required, it is always a good idea to enter the definitive tempo of the finished song into the Mastertrack, in case of accidental changes to the tempo on the Transport bar.

Typically, tempo changes might involve increasing the pace on all the choruses and going back to the original tempo for the verses. This may be achieved by simply manually entering the tempi into the list at the appropriate positions. If certain sections of the tempo changes need to be repeated then copy range in the local Functions menu may be of help (Atari/Falcon version). This copies the Mastertrack data between the left and right locators to a new position according to the current position of the song position pointer. For this operation, the record mode status on the Transport bar, either replace or overdub, will be taken into consideration. With the PC versions of the program standard cut, copy and paste procedures may be used for the general manipulation of data in the Mastertrack.

To really feel what tempi are required in a more musical context try activating 'Record Tempo/Mutes' in the Options menu. If Cubase is then put into record and the tempo changed using the + and − keys of the numeric keypad, each change will be recorded into the Mastertrack. This results in tempo changes which feel more natural and musical. The data may, of course, be edited in the Mastertrack window, as before, but the amount of entries in the list may prove unmanageable, particularly if 16 bars worth of tempi need to be deleted.

The delete facility in the Mastertrack window of the Atari/Falcon version is slightly awkward to use and it may be easier to set the left and right locators to a suitable length of blank space in the song and use Copy Range in replace mode. The song position pointer should be set to the start of the section that needs to be deleted. The result is that all Mastertrack entries for the appropriate section will be replaced with blank space and thus deleted. Of course, when things are just too complicated to handle with the Mastertrack List editor it may be time to use the graphic editor (CueTrax), and many users will prefer the graphic version from the outset.

Synchronization

Cubase provides comprehensive and flexible synchronization features. The program can, of course, run by itself in synchronization with the computer's internal clock but, as with most computer based sequencers, it can also be synchronized to external units.

The main possibilities are as follows:

- The synchronization of Cubase to a tape machine using a time code (SMPTE) interface.
- The synchronization of Cubase to an external device via MIDI Time Code (MTC).
- The synchronization of Cubase to an external device via MIDI Clock.

Selecting Synchronization in the Options menu opens a dialogue where the

Figure 3.8 The
Synchronization dialogue

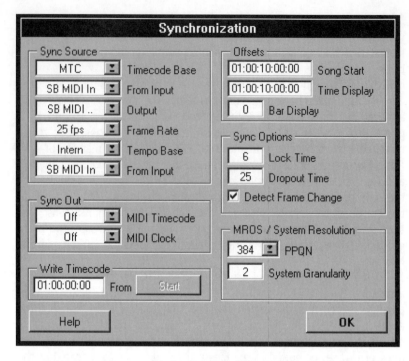

essential parameters may be adjusted (Figure 3.8). In order to have
meaningful interaction with this dialogue, the interface or card being used
must have its driver activated. A driver is a type of file used to provide
Cubase with the necessary data to communicate with an interface.
Steinberg, for example, supply drivers for a number of external Time
Code/MIDI processors such as Midex, Timelock, C-LAB Unitor and SMPII
for the Atari/Falcon platform and the SMPII and MPU401 drivers for the
PC. The PC version of Cubase also supports all devices which are
Windows Multimedia compatible.

With the Atari/Falcon version, a driver is installed by updating its file
extension to make it active (.DR = inactive/.DRV = active). The PC drivers
are installed using special software which comes with the interface or
using the Windows Control Panel. On all platforms, once the driver is
installed, the chosen interface will appear in the Synchronization dialogue
box as one of the options in the relevant pop-up menus of the Sync
Source section.

The default setting of the Synchronization dialogue when Cubase is
supplied is to internal mode, where no synchronization to an external
source is possible. Once adjusted, the synchronization settings are saved
with each Song file.

Synchronizing Cubase to tape using a time code (SMPTE) interface
One of the most reliable methods of synchronizing Cubase to a tape
recorder (or video machine) is to use a time code (SMPTE)
interface/device. This device would be linked to one of the ports of the
computer or, with some MIDI interface cards, would already be installed

inside the PC with synchronization features built in. The time code itself would usually be sent to, and received from, one Track of the tape recorder via send and receive sockets somewhere on the interface.

As a first step, ensure that the interface is correctly linked to the tape machine and the computer, and check, once again, that the appropriate driver has been activated. Before synchronization can occur, the chosen track of the tape machine must be 'striped' with time code i.e.: some kind of time code, (often referred to as SMPTE or EBU time code), must be recorded onto it. Once recorded, this code is played back to the interface which then drives the rest of the system. The interface might convert the time code into MTC, which would then be sent to the computer via a MIDI cable or a virtual MIDI input, or it may provide a direct link to the computer via one of its ports. Let's deal firstly with the direct option. MTC is described further below.

The advantages of using a purpose built synchronization processor like Steinberg's SMPII or SMP24 are, firstly, that the units may be directly controlled from within the software and, secondly, that the accuracy of the synchronization is likely to be better when the unit is connected into the heart of the computer via one of its ports. But most plug in cards with synchronization facilities for the PC are also more than adequate. To synchronize a tape machine to Cubase in this way, proceed as follows:

- Depending on which time code/SMPTE synchronization device is in use, SMPTE code itself may be sent out by remotely activating the 'Write SMPTE/Timecode' option. This initiates the striping of the tape with time code at the rate set in Frame Rate (usually 25 frames per second in Europe) and at the start time set in the Write SMPTE/Timecode box (indicated in hours, minutes, seconds and frames). Stripe the tape.
- Once striping is complete, select the name of the time code/SMPTE device being used in the SMPTE Sync/Timecode Base pop-up of the Sync Source section. This pop-up will also contain 'Intern' and 'MTC' options.
- The 'From input' pop-up contains the names of the currently available input ports. Select the name of the device, which often appears in the list as a virtual port. Cubase will then be expecting to receive time code from this port.
- Select the desired frame rate which should be the same as that which was recorded on the tape.
- Set Tempo Sync/Base to Internal and ignore its 'From input' box.
- Next, select the start time for the song in the Offsets section. This is the time in the received time code which Cubase will treat as the starting point for the song. For certain uses it is appropriate to set time display to the same as the song start. This causes Cubase's main time position on the Transport bar to match the time code which is being received from tape. This is desirable for cases when all machines in the set up need to display the same SMPTE time. Note that the offsets section displays the time in hours, minutes, seconds, frames *and* sub-frames.

TIP

*The Offsets section of the Synchronization dialogue can cause confusion owing to its extra digits of resolution. Remember that the Offsets section displays the time code in hours, minutes, seconds, frames **and** sub-frames.*

- Activate the sync option on the Transport bar, (using the mouse or X on the computer keyboard). Rewind the tape machine to before the start time of the song and put it into play mode. When the interface receives code on or after the song start time, Cubase will go into play mode, synchronized with the tape.

Those who have already used time code will know that Cubase will automatically chase and lock up to each new tape position selected. The Sync Options dictate exactly how Cubase will lock up to the incoming code as follows:

- Locktime specifies the number of correct frames of time code required before Cubase will lock up to it.
- Dropout time specifies the number of incorrect frames Cubase will tolerate before it drops out of synchronization.
- Detect frame change, when activated, will automatically recognise changes in the frame rate of incoming time code.

Synchronizing Cubase to MIDI Time Code (MTC)

MTC is a particular kind of time code which may be transmitted through an ordinary MIDI cable. The device which sends the MTC to Cubase might be a SMPTE to MTC converter or, perhaps, another sequencer. To synchronize Cubase to MTC set up the synchronization dialogue as follows:

- Set SMPTE Sync/Timecode Base to MTC.
- Select the MIDI port which will be receiving MTC in the 'From input' pop-up.
- Set Tempo Sync to 'Internal'.
- Select the appropriate frame rate and activate sync on the transport bar.
- Cubase may now be synchronized to the external unit using MTC, and the handling will be much the same as with ordinary time code. The external unit will very often be a SMPTE to MTC converter, much like the first instance above. If this is the case, the user should have striped the tape, as before.

Remember that, on average, MTC adds 12% to the load in the MIDI cable. This means that, in critical timing situations, it could interfere with other data or, more importantly, other data could interfere with it. If possible, send the MTC into the computer on its own exclusive MIDI cable. This would normally require an interface with two MIDI inputs. However, for all but the most extreme of applications, MTC merged with other data on the same MIDI input is a perfectly adequate solution.

Note that both the time code (SMPTE) Interface and MTC synchronization options do not dictate the actual tempo of Cubase. This is still governed by the tempo indicated on the Transport bar or by the tempo (or tempo changes) in the Mastertrack, when it is activated. However, synchronizing Cubase using MIDI Clock is a different story.

Synchronizing Cubase to MIDI Clock

MIDI Clock data contains messages called song position pointers, as well as tempo information, to keep Cubase in sync with an external unit. The external unit could be a time code to MIDI converter or another sequencer. To synchronize Cubase to MIDI Clock, set up the synchronization dialogue as follows:

- In the synchronize box, set SMPTE Sync/Timecode Base to 'Internal'.
- In the Tempo Sync/Base pop-up select 'MIDI Clock'.
- In the From input of the Tempo Sync/Base section, select the MIDI input into which the MIDI Clocks are being fed.
- This time the external unit governs the basic tempo and any tempo changes of Cubase. Therefore, any tempo changes programmed into the song will have to be re-programmed into the controlling device, which has become a kind of external mastertrack.

Synchronization to MIDI Clock is rather awkward and inconvenient when compared with the other synchronization methods. However, it is a useful addition to the synchronization toolbox. For example, once Cubase is locked to SMPTE/EBU Time code or MIDI Time Code, MIDI Clock could be sent out using the Sync Out option to drive any slaved MIDI devices in the system. It is advisable to drive a MIDI system where time code to MIDI conversion is occurring at only one point, thus minimising the possibility of sychronization errors.

Modular matters

The contents of the Modules menu will vary according to which version and platform is being used. As explained in Chapter 1, modules are self-contained segments of the system which can be hooked on when required and jettisoned when not in use, in order to conserve RAM memory.

The MIDI Processor is just such a module. It comes with most versions of the program and serves as a good example. Like all modules it must first be available and active in the modules selector in order to use it.

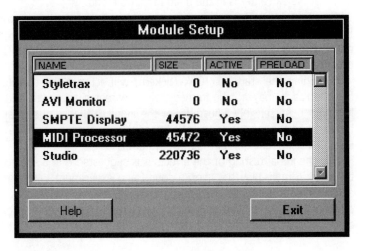

Figure 3.9 The Modules selector

Selecting 'Setup', (or 'Modules'), from the Modules menu opens the Modules selector which features four columns indicating the module name, its size, its active status and its preload status (Figure 3.9). Modules will already be present if they have been put in the modules directory. Atari/Falcon modules should have a .MOD file extension and PC modules should have a .DLL file extension. The modules are automatically added to the modules selector list when Cubase is started.

A typical Atari/Falcon modules list might include any combination of the General MIDI menu, the File selector, the Arpeggiator, the SysEx editor, Score edit, the MIDI Processor, the IPS module or the MIDI Mixer.

Mac and PC versions would feature a very different modules list, including Styletrax, AVI Monitor, SMPTE Display, the MIDI Processor and the Studio Module. The Mac and PC Score edit and Cuetrax are not classed as modules at all but are found instead in other parts of the program.

Further modules may be added to the list using the Add button, which opens the File dialogue, and modules may be deleted from the list using the 'Remove' button (Atari/Falcon version). However, a module is not actually residing in memory until it has been activated. This is achieved by selecting the desired module and clicking in its Active column.

The user may set modules to automatically load into memory each time the program is started by clicking in the Preload/Autoload column. This actually writes the autoload status to the module file itself. A module which has its Preload/Autoload status on will always be automatically loaded into memory (be made active) upon starting the program and, if added to the list later, this too will be loaded directly into RAM memory.

Setting up the MIDI Processor module

So let's first activate the MIDI Processor module. Note that, at this stage, the MIDI Processor itself is not actually being opened. Once activated, the modules themselves may be found in a variety of other menus and locations depending on their function and it will not always be obvious that they are modules at all. Once activated, the MIDI Processor itself is selected from the extra items in the main Modules menu.

Selecting MIDI Processor from the Modules menu opens the MIDI Processor window (Figure 3.10). This manipulates MIDI data to produce delay, chorus and pitch-shift effects. The window has an on/off status box, input and output selectors and six sliders.

Switching the status to 'On', (ticked), will activate the current effect but the result may not be immediately apparent if the input and output have not been sensibly adjusted. Set the input to that of the master keyboard , and the output to the MIDI channel and output port of a synthesizer or rackmount unit in the MIDI system.

For the initial testing of the effects it is suggested that a snare drum is targeted. Simply play the chosen sound and experiment with the repeat and echo sliders to produce echo and delay effects. The sliders may be directly dragged, moved coarsely by clicking above or below the slider control, or adjusted directly in each slider's value box.

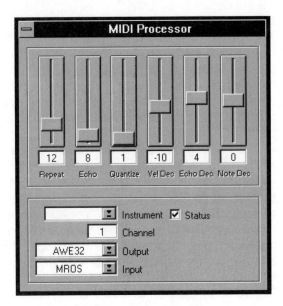

Figure 3.10 The MIDI Processor

- *Repeat* sets the number of repeats desired from each incoming note event.
- *Echo* sets the delay time between each repeat with one unit of the slider representing eight ticks.
- *Quantize* moves the repeats to the nearest set value (one unit, once again representing eight ticks).
- *Echo Dec* adds or subtracts a set number (8 ticks per unit) for each subsequent repeat to produce accelerated or decelerated echo effects.
- *Vel Dec* adds or subtracts a set velocity value for each subsequent repeat to produce crescendo or de-crescendo echoes.
- *Note Dec* adds or subtracts from the note value of each subsequent repeat to produce arpeggio-like effects.

In order to guide the user the table shows various echo and quantize slider values and their corresponding note values:

MIDI Processor slider values

MIDI Processor Slider	No. of ticks	Note value
48	384	1/4 note
24	192	1/8 note
16	128	1/8 triplet
12	96	1/16 note
8	64	1/16 triplet
6	48	1/32 note
4	32	1/32 triplet
3	24	1/64 note

Using the MIDI Processor module

That's a start in understanding the functions of the MIDI Processor, but how do we process a recorded Track ? This requires a little knowledge of the possibilities of MROS (MIDI Real Time Operating System). Most Steinberg products run under MROS which provides synchronization and connection possibilities between different programs running on the same computer. But it also provides the possibility of sending data to different parts of the same system.

If the Arrange window output column of the target Track is set to MROS and the MIDI Processor's input is set to MROS, it will then receive and process the MIDI data of the chosen Track. It may also be necessary to reset the MIDI Processor Output to send the processed data to the appropriate unit. It's rather like an internal patching system.

We could now take things one stage further and consider what needs to be set in order to actually record the output of the MIDI Processor. In this case, set the output to MROS and then go into the MIDI Setup dialogue box (as described at the beginning of this Chapter), and set the 'Record from' box to MROS. This patches the output of the MIDI Processor to the record input of Cubase and all data output from the MIDI Processor may be recorded on an appropriate Track. Remember that, once the MIDI Processor is 'On', it is possible to leave the window and work freely in other areas of the program; the MIDI Processor will still be functioning.

The MIDI Processor may be handy for those users not possessing vast numbers of effects units, but remember that it can also produce effects difficult to achieve on conventional units. However, since the processing relies upon adding to existing MIDI note data, it could, in certain circumstances, produce undesirable hold-ups in the data flow of the rest of the music. It all depends on the density of the other events in the arrangement. Nevertheless, it is well worth spending some time exploring the possibilities.

Try the following settings as starting points for your own experiments:

MIDI Processor starting points

Repeat	Echo	Quantize	Velocity dec	Echo dec	Note dec
2	4	5	-10	0	0
3	8	1	-30	-2	0
4	48	1	-30	-12	0
12	8	1	-10	4	0
3	12	1	6	0	5
4	12	1	0	0	12

That is just one of the modules available but users requiring extra features should find the others on the list well worth exploring. For example, the SMPTE Display Module provides a very usable and practical large digit time code display for time critical situations and the Studio Module is a must for bringing a complex MIDI setup under central control.

Input Transformation

The MIDI Setup and MIDI Filter dialogues control the real-time transformation of data as it arrives at the input of Cubase. The Input Transformation dialogue (Options menu) also operates on input data in real-time, but provides a more comprehensive range of possibilities.

The Input Transformation window (Figure 3.11) closely resembles the Logical edit window in easy mode. Its functions are to either transform or filter incoming data according to the settings of the Filter and Processing sections. Transform and Filter mode are found in the Functions box in the lower part of the window. Filter ignores the Processing part of the window while Transform takes all settings into account.

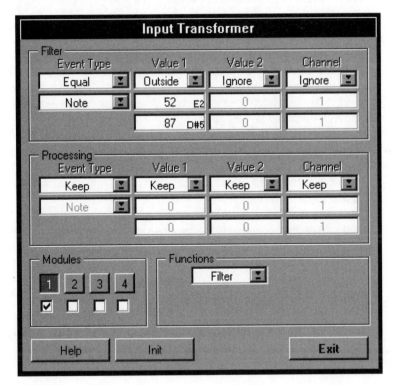

Figure 3.11 The Input Transformer

A statement in plain English describing a simple filtering action in the window might run as follows :

IF the input data contains aftertouch messages THEN filter them

This translates into the window as follows:

- In the Filter section, set the event type column to read 'equal Aftertouch' with all other columns being ignored.
- Ignore the Processing section.
- Choose Filter as the function mode.

In Filter mode the Processing section would not be active. The result would simply be the stripping of all aftertouch messages from the incoming data. Similarly a transformation setting might be described as follows:

IF the input data contains control change 1 messages (Modulation)
THEN change (fix) this data to control change 7 messages (Volume)

This translates as follows:

- In the Filter section, set the event type to equal 'Control Change' and the value 1 column to 'equal 1'.
- In the Processing section. set the value 1 column to 'fix 7'
- Set the mode to Transform in the Functions box.

The result would be the transformation of any modulation messages (control change 1) into volume messages (control change 7).

So, as we can see, the logic of the window may be expressed as a kind of IF,THEN statement, as found in computer languages. Take a look in the pop-up menus of the various columns and it becomes clear that some very sophisticated filtering and transformation actions are possible. In addition, the window offers the possibility of four transformation set-ups in its memory at the same time (presets 1 – 4), and activating (ticked) or de-activating (unticked) any combination. Note that the data travels through each activated filter/transformation setup in its numbered order, so messages filtered out of setup number 1 would not reach setup number 2 and so on.

The contents of the Input Transformer are saved with the song. The Definition files that come with the program already contain four presets which are useful for understanding the possibilities but you may also like to try the two following examples.

Setting a filter to restrict the input range of an instrument
For the playing range of a trumpet, for example, proceed as follows:

- In the Filter section, set the event type column to 'equal note' and the value 1 column to 'Outside 52 (E2) to 87 (D#5)'.
- Set the mode to Filter in the Functions box.

The result would be the filtering of any notes outside the chosen range. This kind of filter is excellent for keeping within the natural note range of an instrument, if a sense of realism is what your arrangement needs. It would also curb the dubious desires of the crazed soloist who insists on playing outside the instrument's natural range.

Changing pitch bend into pan data

To set a transformation which changes pitch bend into pan data:

- Set the Filter event type column to 'equal pitch bend'.
- Set the Processing section event type column to 'fix control change' and the value 1 column to 'fix 10' (Pan controller).

The result would be the immediate transformation of any pitch bend messages into pan data. This setup is excellent for the inspired real-time application of pan data using the synth's pitch wheel, which is a natural choice for manipulating pan.

Of course, many more configurations are possible and, by using two or more setups simultaneously, the user can design extremely complex filters and data transformations. And remember that any efforts made here will serve you well if ever you decide to venture into Logical edit.

Other useful features

Transpose/Velocity

Transpose/Velocity, (selected in the Functions menu or with ctrl + H on the computer keyboard), is for the manipulation of the pitch and velocity of notes. When selected, a small window presents options to change either the pitch or the velocity or both at the same time (Figure 3.12).

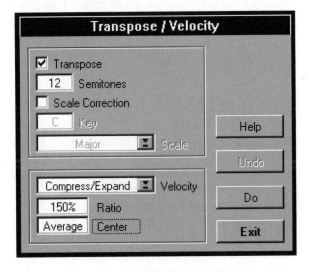

Figure 3.12 The Transpose/Velocity dialogue

Transpose
The Transpose section pitch shifts the chosen data up or down in semitones. Data may also be corrected according to a number of chosen scales using the scale correction option.

Velocity
The Velocity options are slightly more complicated. These include the following:

- the addition or subtraction of a set velocity amount from all chosen notes.
- the limiting of velocities between a set lower and upper limit (this lowers or raises any velocities outside of the set range without affecting those within it).
- the compression/expansion of velocities according to a percentage and a centre point (Average). This requires some explanation. The compression/expansion ratio is in the range -100% to +300%. Ratios above 100% will produce expansion and those below 100% will produce compression. The centre setting is used to calculate from where the expansion or compression will occur. It may be set to average, where the program finds its own centre value based on an average of the velocities of the chosen data, or it may be set to any user value. Velocities with exactly the centre value will not be affected by the operation. On expansion, all velocity values lower than centre will be lowered and all those above will be raised, both according to the percentage amount. On compression, all velocity values lower than centre will be raised and all those above will be lowered, once again both according to the percentage amount.

Remember that Transpose/Velocity produces a permanent effect on the data but this may be undone as long as the edit remains in the clipboard. As a general precaution, it is probably best to work with Transpose/ Velocity from within one of the editors until the options have been mastered thoroughly. In this way, any updates to the data will only be committed to memory when leaving the editor using 'keep'. In the case of an undesirable result, using 'cancel' to leave the editor will return the Part to its original form.

The Note Pad

The Note Pad (Figure 3.13), found in the Edit menu or opened using ctrl + B, is one of those Cubase features for which it is difficult to find a good use. But how many times have you loaded up versions of the same song which are subtly different but you can't remember why, and you can't remember which one is the definitive version? Simply entering some explanatory text into the Note Pad could have saved a lot of time and ensured that the definitive arrangement had been loaded. The Note Pad is Cubase's own mini word processor and as well as entering guide text, as above, could also be used to note:

- Special settings or patches used in a song.
- The dates and times when the song was worked on.
- The track listing for the multitrack tape tracks.
- The administrative details of the song, such as the names of the composer/writer or the record/publishing company.

The contents of the Note Pad are saved with each separate arrangement.

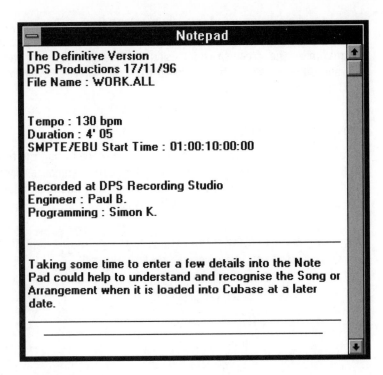

Figure 3.13 The Note Pad

Part Appearance

Another miscellaneous function of Cubase is Part Appearance found in the Options menu. This is a facility to manage the appearance of Parts in the Arrange window. The selection of this item brings up the choice of 'show frames', 'show names' or 'show events'. The first shows the Parts in the Arrange window as blank strips, the second shows the Parts with names and the third shows the events contained in the Parts as vertical lines.

Not only can all events be shown, it is also possible to visually filter the event types by ticking only those required. This is excellent for searching for specific events in a complicated arrangement. It is also useful for seeking out melodies and is invaluable in giving a more detailed overview of the actual contents of an arrangement.

The Windows menu

The Windows menu is another Cubase feature which is easily overlooked. It can, however, prove very handy for those users needing to look at data in several windows at the same time. This concept will already be very familiar to PC users, but this multi-window capacity is available on all platforms.

The ability to tile several editors onto the same screen can be invaluable when editing data in fine detail. Simply hold shift when opening each respective editor (alt on the Atari/Falcon version), and then select 'tile' from the Windows menu to see two or more editors on screen simultaneously. In addition, the Windows menu is where the user may select the

Arrangement from the listed Arrangements currently in memory. The Windows menu also allows the user to hide or show the transport bar. This maximises the screen space for using the Arrange window or the editors, and Cubase may still be controlled from the numeric keypad where the Transport bar functions are replicated.

More smart moves

The features outlined in this chapter are often managed using the mouse but there are still a substantial number of keyboard commands, particularly for the quantize functions, which help speed things up. The following table outlines some of the most useful keyboard moves.

Computer keyboard	Function
Q	Over quantize
W	Note On quantize
E	Iterative quantize
J	Groove quantize
U	Undo quantize
1 – 7	set quantize value
T	set triplet quantize value
.	set dotted quantize value
X	Synchronization on/off
M	Mastertrack on/off
ctrl + M	open Mastertrack
ctrl + H	open Transpose/Velocity dialogue
ctrl + K	repeat Part(s) dialogue
ctrl + B	open Note Pad
alt (+ ctrl) + F	Freeze Playback Parameters

Having got this far, you should now be a reasonable user of Cubase. Indeed, you may already have all the knowledge you need to get successful results from the system. The next two chapters go on to explore some of the more specialist features of the program.

4

A practical introduction to Score edit

More than any other part of Cubase, Score edit is a world unto itself and is a truly major feature of the program. Yet, as you may have already realised, it is not necessary to understand Score edit in order to use Cubase. However, to use Score edit itself, an understanding of Score's particular way of functioning is essential, and some knowledge of musical theory is a pre-requisite. (This chapter outlines the features of the Cubase Score version of the program and other versions may vary in the options available.)

Background

Primarily, we will need to manipulate notes on a virtual score sheet but, unlike the other editors, we will also need to tell Score edit how to interpret the data. If the written score were to exactly follow the nuances of most musical performances, the result would be absurdly difficult to read. The design principle involves the MIDI data on one side and the score on the other, with the user in the middle ensuring that it all makes intelligent musical sense. Those not familiar with musical theory will obviously encounter some difficulty here and must read up on the subject elsewhere. Those who already know some of the basics should be able to manage by conducting their own visual and aural experiments in Score edit.

Similarly to the other editors, pre-recorded musical data may be viewed and updated, but Score edit is also designed for the direct scoring of arrangements within the window alone. Of course, by its very nature, Score edit is disposed towards the editing of notes but it also deals with special score events. Also, in complete contrast to any other part of Cubase, Score edit can print out the music as a full and professional score sheet. This could be anything from an entire orchestral arrangement to a basic lead sheet. Whatever your scoring needs, Score edit can usually fulfil them but, as with most things that are worthwhile, there is a learning curve.

Ways of using Score edit include the following:

- To produce a printed version of the recorded musical data.
- To act as the main editor for the recorded musical data with no regard for any potential printout of the material.

- To enter notes directly onto the score (in step-time or by adding to a blank score), to be printed out at a later stage.
- To enter notes directly onto the score, (in step-time or by adding to a blank score), to be played back via MIDI at a later stage.

Data may have been recorded in Score edit via MIDI or via the manual writing of notes onto the score. The manually entered case would often be tested by sending the data out via MIDI. This is excellent for testing complex pre-written scores and allows the orchestral arranger the luxury of testing the work before presenting it to the live orchestra. Whichever way Score edit is being used, there are some essential elements which mark it apart from the other editors: it has two modes, 'Edit mode' and 'Page mode' and it features something called 'Display Quantize'.

Before going on to explanations of these let's first get to know the Score edit window in Page mode. Page mode has the same editing features as Edit mode but provides additional functions for the printing and visual processing of the score.

A quick look around

Choose a simple Part or several Parts in any arrangement and open Score edit by selecting it from the Edit menu or pressing ctrl + R on the computer keyboard. The Mac and PC versions feature Score edit already loaded as a standard part of the program but the Atari/Falcon version's Score edit is classed as a module and will need to be activated before using the editor. Once Page mode has been selected from the Score menu (Atari/Falcon – Option menu), the window should resemble Figure 4.1, (without the help boxes, of course). Score edit toggles between Edit mode and Page mode. Remember that the appearance of the page will also depend on what was initially selected in the arrange Window. Staves are arranged as a grand staff featuring the names of each Track (corresponding to the chosen Parts) in the same order as they were found in the Arrange window Track List.

Working down the screen (Figure 4.1), there is the usual title bar, showing the name of the Part and its bar range, a two line function/status bar, an Info Line, a toolbar, and the Score display. There are the usual horizontal and vertical scroll bars at the bottom and right of the window plus an additional scale selector, a page selector, a show/hide toolbar icon and a show/hide status bar icon in the bottom right area.

Note also the pop-up toolbox (click right mouse) which features new tools unique to Score edit. In the Atari/Falcon version, open the local 'Function', 'Staff', 'Format' and 'Option' menus to glimpse the comprehensive range of features for the manipulation of all kinds of score data. In the Mac and PC versions, the same features are available in the main Score menu which becomes active when Score edit is selected.

Some of the most important features are reproduced on the toolbar found just below the usual Info line. The toolbar includes, (from left to right):

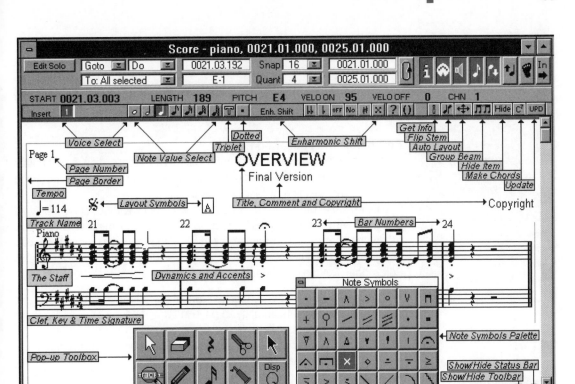

Figure 4.1 Score edit overview

- 'Voice select' when working with polyphonic voicings.
- 'Note value select' with triplet and dotted options.
- 'Enharmonic shift' for selecting appropriate accidentals.
- the 'Get info' button for opening a suitable pop-up dialogue for selected score items.
- the 'Flip stem' button for reversing the direction of the stems of selected notes.
- the 'Auto layout' button for automatically formatting the score and layout according to the 'Global' and 'Staff Settings' dialogues.
- the 'Group beam' button for joining or breaking the beam between quavers, semiquavers etc.
- the 'Hide item' button for hiding any chosen item(s) in the Score.
- the 'Make chords' button for automatic chord creation.
- the 'Force update' button to force a screen redraw.

The Score window obviously normally includes the staff with the Track name, default clef and the current time signature. The key would normally have to be manually selected by the user in the 'Staff Settings' dialogue, (Atari/Falcon – 'Staff' menu), at which time some of the accidentals on notes in the default staff might disappear. The staff could also include a tempo indication, bar numbers and a variety of layout symbols and dynamics and accent markings.

In addition, the Page mode screen would feature a page number and page border, and standard title, comment and copyright headings at the

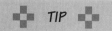
top of the first page. Some of these may not always be visible since the page is formatted according to the way things have been set up in 'Global Settings' (Atari/Falcon – Option Menu).

The modes of operation and Display Quantize

Edit mode and Page mode

That completes a quick look around but before proceeding further let's take some time to understand the differences between Edit and Page mode and the meaning of Display Quantize.

The essential difference between the two modes is that Page mode was designed with a final *printed* version of the score in mind whereas Edit mode does not deal with this aspect at all. Page mode has more functions and possibilities but still performs all the editing operations available in Edit mode. The main differences are as follows:

- The Score edit window scrolls horizontally in Edit mode but scrolls vertically and flips from page to page in Page mode.
- The layout symbols palette is not available in Edit mode.
- The layout pointer tool is not available in Edit mode's pop-up toolbox.
- 'Hide' does not function in Edit mode.
- 'Auto layout' is not applicable in Edit mode.
- There is no title, comment and copyright in Edit mode.
- Magnification is not available in Edit mode.
- Printing is not possible in Edit mode.

Display Quantize

As well as the two modes Score edit also features the concept of 'Display Quantize' (found in the 'Staff Settings' dialogue or managed with the display quantize tool). In general, Cubase is concerned with an aural result but Score edit, particularly in Page mode, is also concerned with a quality visual representation.

You may already be familiar with the term WYSIWYG, meaning 'What you see Is what you get'. This could be applied to Score edit in Page mode since what you see is, more or less, what you get, except for the sometimes jagged text with the Atari/Falcon version (which actually gets printed out in better quality). However, if you attempt to apply WYSIWYG to Score edit in an aural sense then things become confusing. Most finished scores produced from an actual musical performance do not sound the same as they appear. This is due to 'Display Quantize'.

Display Quantize adjusts the graphic positions and values of the notes in the score without affecting the aural result. This preserves the musicality of a performance which, if displayed exactly as played, would be intolerable in the written score sense. Display Quantize is explained in more detail below.

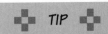

Becoming familiar

There now follows a very brief tutorial on some of the basic aspects of Score edit. At this stage, we do not need to be particularly concerned about creating a meaningful score since we are just becoming familiar with what is available. So relax and let yourself go. However, always work on a *copy* of the Song or Arrangement until Score edit becomes more familiar.

Select Page mode

First, select Page mode from the main menu, (Atari/Falcon – Option menu), and switch back and forth with Edit mode to become familiar with the differences. For example, it will be noticed immediately that Edit mode presents the score without a title.

Title, comment and copyright

Stay in Page mode and double click with the left mouse button on the title. This opens the 'Title, comment and copyright' dialogue where the appropriate information may be typed in. Type something for each section and click on OK to go back to the score.

CLICK ON PENCIL FIRST

Select tempo

Next open the 'Symbol Palettes' from the Score menu, (Atari/Falcon – select 'Symbols' on the status bar). Select any palette. At the top of the palette is the name of the current group of symbols, click on this to view the menu of the other available palettes. Select 'Other', (Atari/Falcon – 'Symbols 2' selected by clicking on the palette name to open a pop-up menu), and then select the Tempo symbol (represented as a crotchet followed by the tempo) which will already be set to the current tempo of Cubase. Upon selection, the mouse pointer will change into the pencil tool and by clicking in the appropriate area at the beginning of the staff the tempo icon will be inserted into the score.

NO - choose pencil for tool bar

Insert symbols

Try inserting symbols from any of the palettes and position them appropriately into the score, (each time the pointer will change into the pencil). *NOT TRUE* The symbols which are note specific, such as accent, staccato and dynamic ornamentation, may be attached to specific note positions by clicking upon the chosen note itself. If a note is not chosen, the symbol will be placed at the nearest note found along the staff. Most text, layout and other symbols may be placed virtually anywhere on the page. After entry, any symbol may be later dragged to a new position, updated, deleted or copied in standard Cubase fashion. *How?*

Locate specific score segments

Also, try re-locating the song position pointer by clicking with the right mouse button while holding 'alt'. This is useful for locating and playing specific segments of the score.

✦ TIP ✦

If a finished printed version of the score is required it is recommended that a copy is always used which is loaded and saved under a different filename.

tempo
♩ : XX

♩ = 38

The toolbox

You will already be familiar with some of the tools in the toolbox, which is opened in standard Cubase fashion by clicking in white space with the right mouse button. Score edit contains more tools than the other editors and the function of each is as follows.

The pointer tool

Used for selecting, dragging and manipulating specific notes or events (or several at the same time using a stretch box) and the general selection and control of menu items, staves, bar lines, button controls, scroll position, dialogue boxes etc.

The eraser tool

Predictably, behaves like the real physical version, deleting several items if passed over them with the left mouse button held or deleting one at a time with single clicks. It may also be used to delete connecting bar lines between staves.

The rest tool

Used to insert rests into the score at the current value shown in the quantize box. i.e. a value of 4 will insert crotchet (1/4 note) rests. Note that inserting rests in the middle of a score pushes all events which come after it to the right, regardless of the status of the Insert button on the status bar.

The scissors tool

Used to divide a tied note into two separate notes by clicking on the second note head. It may also be used to send the last bar of one staff to the following staff by clicking on the penultimate bar line.

The layout tool

Available in Page mode, may be used to affect the score purely graphically, such as to move a clef without affecting the positions of notes on the staff, to move the graphical order of notes without affecting the order in which they are played back via MIDI, or to adjust the graphical position of slurs and ties without affecting their relationship with the notes to which they are attached.

The magnifying glass

Similar to the other editors, is used to inspect the notes of the score by playing them via MIDI when the tool is passed over them with the left mouse button held or clicked.

The pencil tool

Used to write in all text, ornamentation and other symbols (everything except notes) onto the score and is auto selected when certain symbols have been chosen.

The note tool

Used to write notes onto the score and is auto selected when a note value selection is made. The note tool itself changes to the appropriate note symbol (minim, crotchet, quaver etc.) according to the note value selection.

The glue tool

Used to join consecutive notes of the same pitch as in the other editors. It may also be used to connect bar lines between staves and to bring a bar up from the following staff by clicking on the last bar line of the upper staff.

The display quantize tool

Used to insert new display quantize settings at specific positions along the staff when processing particularly complicated passages within a score. This gives complete control over the score appearance and overcomes almost all difficulties encountered in the display of complex material.

The handling of notes

Obviously, among the most important elements of any score are the notes (and rests) themselves. Score edit provides for just about any possible note editing requirement. Notes are usually manipulated using the mouse and various tools from the toolbox. This manipulation comes in six essential forms: selecting, moving, copying, deleting, updating (editing) and adding (inserting) as follows.

Selecting

Notes may be selected one at a time by choosing the pointer tool and clicking on each with the left mouse button. Multi selections may be made by holding the shift key while doing this. A single note among a multi selection may be de-selected by holding 'shift' and re-clicking on it.

Several notes may be simultaneously selected by drawing a stretch box over the desired events by clicking and dragging in white space (similar to the other editors) and then stretching the graphic box over the desired note heads. Double clicking with the left mouse while holding 'alt' selects all notes of the same pitch on all octaves. Double clicking with the left mouse while holding 'ctrl' selects all notes of the same pitch and the same octave.

In addition, notes may be stepped through using the left and right arrows of the computer keyboard with or without 'shift' to multi select or not. Selections may be made on one or several staves at the same time. The heads of selected notes change to reverse video and may be easily recognised on the screen. As in the other editors, if individual notes are to be played via MIDI as each is selected then the loudspeaker icon in the status bar should be highlighted.

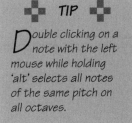

❖ TIP ❖

Double clicking on a note with the left mouse while holding 'alt' selects all notes of the same pitch on all octaves.

Moving

Notes may be moved individually by clicking, holding and dragging with the left mouse button or in groups by clicking, holding and dragging on one of the selected group. As usual, notes will be dropped at their new destination according to the current Snap value.

Notes may be moved up or down in pitch, or left or right along the staff, or between staves, as desired. Before releasing, notes will be magnetic to the current Snap value and, if 'ctrl' is held down, changes in pitch will only be within the scale of the current key signature. Cut, copy and paste actions are useful for moving larger blocks of data around. Data moved to the clipboard using cut may be pasted to the current song position pointer in the active staff.

Copying

Notes may be copied in standard Cubase fashion by pressing 'alt' on the computer keyboard while clicking, holding and dragging on a note or group of notes with the left mouse button. The copy which appears may be manipulated in position and pitch, as with 'Moving' above, and, once again, notes will be dropped at their new destination according to the current Snap value. The 'copy' of cut, copy and paste may also be used to copy notes in Score edit.

Deleting

Notes may be deleted by making the appropriate selection using one of the above methods and then pressing delete or backspace on the computer keyboard. Alternative delete actions include clicking on one or more notes with the eraser tool and using delete from the Do menu, (Atari/Falcon – Function menu), after having selected the appropriate notes. Remember that when notes are deleted they are automatically replaced in the score by the appropriate rest.

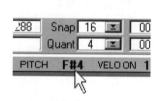

Updating

Note selections may also be updated and edited in a number of other ways. Similarly to the other editors, the characteristics of the selected note appear on the Info bar near the top of the screen. Any of the parameters may be decreased or increased using the left and right mouse buttons. This obviously includes changing the position in time or the length and pitch of the note. Selections may also be updated via MIDI if the MIDI icon and the appropriate combination of note, Note On velocity and Note Off velocity icons is selected. Cubase automatically steps on to the next note after each entry.

Other editing techniques include the joining together of consecutive notes of the same pitch using the glue tool and separating tied notes using the scissors. Holding alt while clicking on a note head with the note tool will change its length to the current quantize length in the quantize box.

Adding

Notes may be added anywhere on the score using the note tool. The note tool will be automatically selected when one of the note value symbols is selected on the toolbar and the note may be inserted anywhere on the staves. The note value may be selected using the mouse or numbers 1-7 on the computer keyboard.

Click on the staff with the note tool and do not release until the desired pitch and position have been found. The unreleased note will be magnetic to the current Snap value and the precise pitch may be verified in the 'Pitch' parameter of the Info bar. Notes may be restricted to the current key if 'ctrl' is held down at the time of entry. Notes are always *added* to the score unless the Insert icon of the status bar is selected, in which case all notes which come after the entry will be pushed to the right.

That covers most of the possibilities with notes in Score edit. Rests are managed similarly but when they are entered onto the score the data which comes after them is *always* pushed to the right regardless of the status of the Insert icon.

INFO

The rest tool is used similarly to the note tool and its value is managed, once again, by using the mouse to select the note values on the toolbar or by pressing the computer keyboard numbers 1-7.

Project 1

Creating a piano score

Let's start using Score edit in earnest by creating a simple piano score. The object of this exercise is to finish up with a well presented, readable score on a split staff with some kind of ornamentation or markings suggesting how it should be played. The score will then be printed. *Always* work on a copy, to avoid any danger of destroying valuable material.

Figure 4.2 Piano score before editing

piano

Select a Track or a Part in the Arrange window which is for a piano or a related keyboard instrument. To illustrate the procedure here a very simple 4 bar piano part playing chords was chosen (see Figure 4.3). With the Part selected, open Score edit from the Edit menu or use ctrl + R. The notes will almost certainly appear in a format which is not acceptable for a piano score, with no split staff and perhaps an inappropriate display quantize setting (see unedited score Figure 4.2). Also, if the music is in any key other than C major there will invariably be some accidentals. Taking the illustrated piano part as an example, the following steps need to be taken to make things acceptable:

Figure 4.3 Piano score after editing

Set title details

Change the mode to Page mode and double click on the title. A dialogue box will appear where a suitable title, comment and copyright may be entered (Figure 4.4). It is also possible to change the size and font of the text from within the dialogue.

Figure 4.4. The Title, Comment and Copyright dialogue

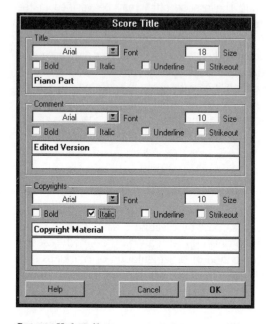

Set staff details

Open the Staff Settings dialogue (Figure 4.5). This provides the most important parameters for obtaining a legible score. The first item in the dialogue box is 'Staff mode'. Set this to 'Split' and ensure that the split point is set to C3 (middle C). Click on OK to approve the changes and go back to the score. Things should already be looking a little better.

Figure 4.5. The staff settings dialogue with the staff options dialogue

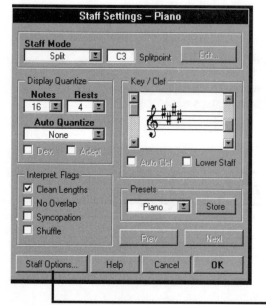

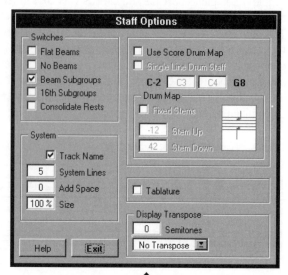

Set other symbols

Open the Symbols palette and select 'Other' (Atari/Falcon – 'Symbols 2'). Select the tempo indicator and either drag it onto the score and release at the appropriate position on the staff, or select it and click on the appropriate position using the pencil tool (which automatically appears when certain types of symbols are chosen).

Select Global settings

Open 'Global settings' and select 'Bars' from the topic list (Figure 4.6). Set the 'Bar numbers every' box to 'Off' so that bar numbers will not be displayed on the score. Set 'Default bars across the page' to 4 – Score edit will display four bars across the page, if it is practical. While in Global settings select 'Page Numbers' from the topic list and ensure that the active box is *not* ticked. In this case, page numbers will not be displayed. Click on OK to leave the dialogue box. You may need to use the Auto Layout button to take into account all the new global settings.

Figure 4.5(a) Other symbols palette

Figure 4.6 Global Settings Bar dialogue

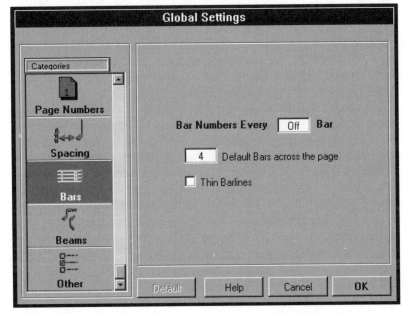

Some confusion may arise with 'Default bars across the page' in Page mode since, unlike Edit mode, changes in the default number are not automatically registered when leaving the global settings dialogue. Clicking the Auto Layout button takes into account the changes.

However, in Page mode, yet another control, 'Number of bars' is also available (Figure 4.7). It is best to use this *after* most other editing has been completed. The Number of Bars dialogue allows the chosen number of bars across the page to be imposed upon either all staves (All), the active staff and all those following (Following), or the active staff only (This). Thus, varying numbers of bars across the page may be imposed at any point in the score.

Figure 4.7. Number of Bars
dialogue

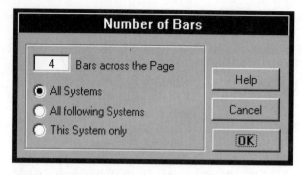

Change the key

The page layout itself is probably now looking much better but, if the score is anything like the example in Figure 4.2, the notes themselves will still be in some disarray. There are many tied notes, awkward dotted rests, short semiquaver rests and numerous accidentals.

The first step to remedy the situation is to insert the correct key. The example is in E major. To change the key, open the Staff Settings dialogue and adjust the key/clef section. The left scroll bar is for clef selection, which we do not need here, and the right scroll bar is for the key. The up scroll arrow selects flat keys and the down scroll arrow selects sharp keys. For the split staff the key will be automatically inserted onto both staves. Select the appropriate key.

The second step, before leaving Staff Settings, is to update the Display Quantize section. This contains note quantize and rest quantize boxes, and a first step to getting the score readable might be setting the note quantize to 16 and the rest quantize to 4, with Auto Quantize set to 'off'.

Below the quantize boxes there are also a number of flags which may be activated by ticking their boxes. Tick 'Clean lengths' and leave the dialogue by clicking on OK. The score will be updated and, if the settings chosen were appropriate, it will be more readable (see the finished score in Figure 4.3).

Check it

Check the score for any incorrect notes. For example, keyboard players sometimes touch the wrong keys when playing chords and, although they are not always audible, they are visible on the score. Bar 2 of the piano part example contains a D# in the E chord which was certainly not intended but did not show up audibly. Such notes should simply be deleted.

Add ornamentation

Add any desired ornamentation from the Symbols palettes. This might include dynamics and accents, and text comments could also be added where appropriate.

Auto format again

Finally, click on the Auto Layout button to reformat the page for a last time and, if all has gone well, the score should resemble the same standard of presentation as that in Figure 4.3.

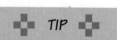

TIP

To change the time signature of a piece simply double click on the existing time signature and enter the new values into the pop-up box. To enter a new time signature use the Clef symbol palette.

Printing the score

When you are satisfied with the result, try printing the score. The printed version should turn out to be as good as, and usually better than, what can be seen on the screen.

Before printing, make sure that Cubase is set up correctly with the choice of printer and that the printer setup options are correctly adjusted.

Printer drivers

Atari/Falcon users should copy the choice of printer file (or driver as it is usually known) to the working disk at the same level as the Cubase Score program, and then change its name to 'DEF.PRN'. However, if a hard disk is being used, this should have already been dealt with as part of the installation procedure. PC users should already have an appropriate default printer selected as part of their Windows setup.

Printer setup

Once set up with the correct printer driver, with the Atari/Falcon version, reboot Cubase and open the 'Printer setup' dialogue box in the File menu. Make sure that paper size is set to A4 and ensure that landscape is *not* ticked so that the print orientation will be portrait. (This tutorial has assumed that the Score page has been set up with the A4 paper size selected in 'Printer Setup', which is the default in this dialogue box when Cubase is supplied. If the Score edit page has been set up with another paper size and this is now changed to A4, the layout of Score edit will need to be reformatted accordingly).

Leave the margins at their default values, (usually 0.30 inches), unless special settings are required. If necessary, a new printer driver may be installed by double clicking on the current printer name.

PC users should make their printing setup adjustments in the 'Print and Page Setup' dialogue of the File menu. The default printer chosen elsewhere in Windows is normally found in the 'Printer' section and the usual page orientation, paper size, margins and other options may be chosen in standard Windows fashion. Figure 4.8 shows a typical 'Print and Page Setup' dialogue.

When everything has been correctly set up and the printer is on line and ready to print, go to the File menu and select Print. This option is available only in Page mode. With the Atari/Falcon version this opens a small dialogue box requesting the page numbers to be printed and the print quality. With 'Fast' ticked the print quality will be draft standard, otherwise it will be a higher quality printout which consequently takes more time.

Printer fonts

Click on OK to activate printing. At this point Cubase may look for certain additional fonts it requires which were not in the CUBASE.DAT folder. This is not the case with a hard disk based system where everything that is required has already been installed, but with diskettes ensure that the

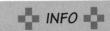

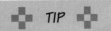

*T*he fonts are important to ensure a high quality printout, avoiding the jagged appearance of certain characters as seen on the computer screen with the Atari/Falcon version. PC users should not encounter such problems since a large selection of fonts will normally already form part of their Windows setup.

Figure 4.8. Printer and Page
Setup dialogue

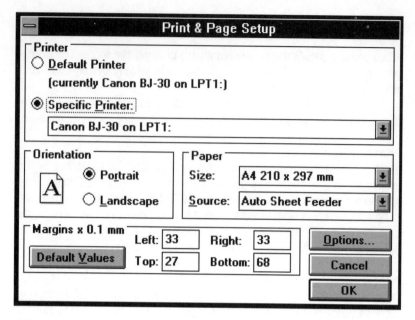

diskette containing the fonts folder is in the drive at the time of printing. A 'Locate the fonts' dialogue box appears. Click on OK and the File selector dialogue appears, where the fonts folder should be opened. Click on OK to leave the File selector.

Once printing goes ahead the Score edit screen will be replaced by intermittent appearances of various enlarged parts of the score and the printer should jump into action. To abort printing simply select and hold the 'esc' key until the Abort dialogue box appears.

Display Quantize in detail

Readers who successfully managed to process and print a score in Project 1 will feel they have made progress but, undoubtedly, some aspects of Score edit will still seem somewhat mysterious. Display Quantize is probably one of these.

Display quantize is sufficiently important to warrant special attention. If the normal quantize functions of Cubase are already understood then Display Quantize will be a little easier to grasp.

Testing Display Quantize

The Display Quantize values, in the Display Quantize section of the Staff Settings dialogue, set the smallest note or rest allowed in the score display. The values are purely for the display and have no effect on the actual MIDI data, which remains as recorded. Without an appropriate setting the display of the notes and rests may appear over complicated and confusing. For example, try recording the following melody into Cubase:

Once recorded, select the new Part in the Arrange window and open Score edit. Assuming that the Part has not been quantized, has been reasonably played, and has display quantize set to 16 for notes and 16 for rests with auto quantize set to off, the melody may initially be displayed more like the following.

Figure 4.9 Test melody

Figure 4.10. The melody with Inappropriate Display Quantize

This apparent confusion in the display will be due to the player's particular manner of expressing the music, such as playing in front of or behind the beat, and possibly real timing errors. Most of the problems will probably revolve around the triplets in bar two. However, if the aural result is satisfactory, changing the note data itself is not a good solution. Display Quantize provides a way of interpreting the playing so that the notes are clearly displayed on the score without disturbing the aural result.

Firstly, let's try entering a note display quantize of 4. As before, do this in the Staff Settings dialogue and make sure that Auto quantize is 'off'. This tells Score edit that the smallest note in the score is a crotchet (1/4 note) and so, in keeping with this, the editor will shift, purely visually, all notes to the nearest crotchet (1/4 note) beat and the score will now resemble something like the following:

Figure 4.11. Too much Display Quantize

The editor has no problem with the first, third and fourth bars since, indeed, the smallest note intended was a crotchet (1/4 note). However, the triplets in bar two now look like chords, and the quavers and semiquavers in bars five and six have also been transformed. The solution might have been to set the note display quantize to the smallest value note which, in this case, is a semiquaver (1/16 note). If there were only 'straight' notes in the passage then this could have worked, but each group of triplets would tend to be displayed as two semiquavers (1/16 notes) and a quaver (1/8 note) because Score edit has been given no guidance on how to interpret them correctly.

The kind of Display Quantize settings chosen depends on the kind of note data to be processed, which can essentially be divided into two groups:

- that which contains a mix of 'straight' AND triplet notes together.
- that which contains 'straight' notes only OR triplets only.

Auto Quantize

One way of processing music containing triplets and 'straight' notes, like the example, is to use 'Auto quantize'. Auto quantize is found in the Staff Settings dialogue just below the main Display Quantize settings. It is either 'off' or in one of two active modes: 'Distance' and 'Position'.

- 'Distance' means that the display quantize will use the distance between the notes to calculate how they should be displayed, without specific regard for their position in time (such as when the playing is behind or ahead of the beat). This is more forgiving of passages which were inaccurately played.
- 'Position', however, is better suited to material which was played more accurately or entered manually. When 'position' is selected, two other options 'Deviation' and 'Adapt' may be toggled on or off. Selecting 'deviation' allows normal detection of notes even if they are not precisely on the beat. This should be turned off for material which has been tightly quantized. 'Adapt' detects the surrounding triplets after one triplet has been found.

Any of these settings could have an undesired effect on the score, so, in all cases, it is better to find out the best option by experimentation. Before using auto quantize always choose the note quantize value first, based on the smallest triplet (for triplet dominated pieces), or the smallest 'straight' note (for pieces containing mainly 'straight' notes).

Using the Display Quantize tool

As an alternative to auto quantize, specific sections of the score could be manually 'display quantized' using the display quantize tool as follows:

- With the display quantize tool selected, (a Q appears on the screen), simply click at the appropriate position along the staff and enter the desired settings into the pop-up box.
- Click on OK to return to the score where the display quantize setting will be shown with a Q followed by the chosen quantize value, such as Q16, for example. This is assuming that display quantize events have not been hidden in 'Show invisible ...' . In addition, if auto quantize has already been used on the staff and a new display quantize setting is later entered with the display quantize tool, any display quantize changes that were invisibly imposed by auto quantize will now be transformed into ordinary visible display quantize settings. This avoids confusion.

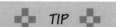

TIP

To process a piece containing 'straight' notes or triplets only, it is better not to use auto quantize. Instead, set the note quantize value to the smallest note in the score and the rest quantize value to the smallest rest required. Ensure that auto quantize reads 'off' and click on OK in the Staff Settings dialogue to go back to the score. Verify that the score makes musical sense and enter any additional display quantize settings using the display quantize tool.

Interpretation flags

In addition to the display quantize settings, the 'Interpretation flags', also found in the Staff Settings dialogue, are particularly useful for various musical styles:

- 'Clean lengths' extends the length of short notes to the next note or rest quantize position and is useful for eliminating the short rests which sometimes appear inappropriately between notes.
- 'No overlap' prevents undesirable strings of ties which sometimes join notes in certain circumstances. Experiment with 'No overlap' whenever unwanted ties become a problem in the score.
- 'Syncopation' may be a better solution than 'No overlap' if ties on long notes which cross the beat have become a problem. Score displays these as two tied notes with 'Syncopation' unticked and a single note with 'Syncopation' ticked.
- The 'Shuffle' flag is designed for a jazz score where 'straight' notes would be used to represent a shuffle beat, in order to make it more legible. A shuffled crotchet triplet (1/4 note triplet) followed by a quaver triplet (1/8 note triplet) become 'straight' quavers (1/8 notes) and a shuffled quaver triplet (1/8 note triplet) followed by a semiquaver triplet (1/16 note triplet) become 'straight' semiquavers (1/16 notes).

Remember that the Interpretation flags may not always be the appropriate solution for display problems on a staff, particularly a long and complicated one. Experimenting with the flags on a trial and error basis is probably the best approach, and always verify the score carefully after use.

The best solution

So now, with all this knowledge in mind, let's go back to the example above. The passage contains triplets *and* 'straight' notes so we could use Auto Quantize or insert display quantize settings using the Display Quantize tool.

A note quantize value of 16, with Auto quantize in 'position' mode and 'deviation' and 'adapt' selected, might be appropriate. Set the rest quantize value to 4, even though there are no rests, and tick the 'Clean lengths' interpretation flag. Some scores may read correctly as in Figure 4.9 above.

However, probably the best method in this case is to set Auto quantize to 'off' and use the display quantize tool. Enter display quantize values of 16 to all but the second bar, which should be set to semiquaver triplets (1/16 note triplets). Tick 'Clean lengths', enter any other appropriate settings and the score should, once again, read correctly (see Figure 4.12).

Figure 4.12. Corrected melody
showing display quantize
symbols

Project 2

Scoring a four part string arrangement

Processing a four part string arrangement in Score edit presents problems not encountered in the first tutorial. Figure 4.13 shows an example of an arrangement before editing. As usual, always work on a duplicate copy of the arrangement to avoid losing important material. It is recommended that you load from, and save to, a file with a different name to the original. This file is used purely for preparing the piece in Score edit. For the purposes of this exercise use Score edit in Page mode.

Figure 4.13 The unedited
string arrangement

Arrange instruments in order

The first task is to arrange the instruments into the correct order in the Arrange window. Simply click, hold and drag the Tracks in the Track list until they are in the correct order. Tracks will appear in Score edit in exactly the same vertical order. Select the Parts required for the score.

The piece could be a short arrangement, as in the example, or an extended score. The example strings arrangement is comprised of four staves; violin I, violin II, cellos and basses in the order in which they might normally be found in an orchestral score. Note that, by default, the staves are displayed as a grand staff with the staves joined by common bar lines.

Decide on the clefs

Next, decide on the clefs required for each staff. The default clef when first opening Score edit is the treble clef. The violins would normally remain with this but the cellos and basses would need to be changed to bass clefs.

This may be achieved in one of two ways. Double click on the clef itself and adjust the clef type in the pop-up window or open Staff Settings, select the appropriate staff with the 'Previous/next' (Up/down) buttons and change the clef in the 'Key/clef' section.

Set the key

Decide on the key and then open Staff Settings and set the key in the 'Key/clef' section for each staff.

Set bars across page

Open the Global settings dialogue. Select 'bars' from the topic list and enter the desired default bars across the page (initially four bars suits most circumstances) and select bar numbers to appear every four bars. Consider also ticking 'Thin barlines', which will tend to help the notes stand out on the finished printed score.

Select page numbers as active by ticking the 'Active' box in the 'Page numbers' section. Click on OK to leave the Global settings dialogue. Open 'Page mode settings' and tick 'Real book' and 'Staff separators'. 'Real book' means that the clef appears only on the first line of the page and 'Staff separators' puts in an automatic staff separator symbol between each grand staff as it appears down the page.

Enter title details

Double click on the title to open the title, comment and copyright dialogue and enter the appropriate details, as described in the first tutorial.

Musicians' directions

Any number of directions might be required in the score to help the musicians understand how the piece should be played. To this end, Score edit provides four types of text.

Regular text ('Text' in the 'Other' symbols palette)
Regular text is tied to the bar and staff position. If the bar or staff is later moved, the regular text will be moved with it.

Page text ('Page text' in the 'Layout' symbols palette)
Page text is not attached to the staff or bar position and will remain at its original location regardless of changes on the staves. It is treated as part of the general layout (known in Score edit as the 'Layout layer', meaning all non-note specific details of the page).

System text ('System text' in the 'Layout' symbols palette).
System text is also part of the layout layer but, unlike page text, may be tied to a specific staff and bar position. System text is also handy when used in conjunction with the empty graphic box symbol found in the layout palette.

The box may be sized appropriately and will be added to the screen on top of all other objects and staves except system text. The two together provide an excellent facility to highlight particularly important information or directions on the score.

Lyrics ('Lyrics' in the 'Other' symbols palette)
The adding of lyrics is explained in the next project.

All text is input by selecting the appropriate symbol from the Symbols palette and clicking at the desired page or bar position with the pencil tool which appears. A pop-up input box is opened into which the text should be written. Any text may be dragged to a new position using standard click and drag procedures. Similarly to other objects found on the Score, text may be aligned using the align functions found in the Format menu.

Enter Layout symbols

Add any Layout symbols appropriate to the score as found in the Layout palette. This might include some rehearsal markers (like the A and B markers in the finished example, Figure 4.14) or perhaps a coda symbol or sign. If the score includes violins I and II, or other related instruments, try linking the staves with the brackets provided. If part of a larger orchestral score then all the strings could be linked with one large bracket. In addition, try indicating a repeated passage using Repeat Barlines. Double click on the appropriate start and end barlines and select the new style bar line from the Bar Lines pop-up window (Figure 4.15). If a better view of the layout in isolation is required then try selecting 'Layout layer only' from the Score menu (Atari/Falcon – Options menu).

Add accents etc.

Finally, add any desired accents, dynamics, slurs and ties to the score and double check that there are no incorrect notes. Accents, slurs and ties etc. are found in the various palettes.

Many of these symbols are note specific. In other words, they may be attached to specific notes within the score. With the Atari/Falcon version,

Figure 1.1 The final version of the string arrangement

this is indicated by a small note in the top right of the symbol box. With the PC version all symbols in the 'Note Symbols' palette are note specific and are always tied to the selected note. Simply select the symbol and, as usual, the pencil tool will appear automatically on the screen. Then click on the desired note and the symbol will appear automatically positioned at a set distance from the note head.

Figure 4.15 Bar Lines pop-up menu

The symbols in the Dynamics palette are selected in a similar fashion but the crescendo and decrescendo (diminuendo) symbols, for example, are entered onto the score at specific positions along the selected staff and are not linked to notes. Similarly, the ppp to fff dynamics are entered at positions along the staves and are also not linked to notes.

Both accents and dynamic symbols may be made to have a real effect on the actual MIDI data. Accents may be given a MIDI meaning by selecting 'MIDI Meaning' from Global settings (Figure 4.16), or if MIDI Meaning is already active a double click on any relevant accent opens the dialogue box. (Atari/Falcon MIDI Meaning is found in the local Options menu). The accents and marks may be given a percentage increase or decrease in velocity or length which will affect the notes to which they are attached (assuming that active is ticked in the dialogue). It is probably best to set up all MIDI Meaning values *before* entering the symbols onto the score, since the results may become confusing if notes are edited and re-edited several times.

Figure 4.16. The MIDI Meaning dialogue

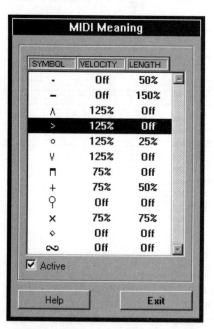

Double clicking on any of the relevant dynamic symbols opens a dialogue box where the range and percentage of the effect may be adjusted. For example, a crescendo may be given a start and end position and a velocity range, which will effect the target notes accordingly (Figure 4.17).

There is one important difference between MIDI Meaning processing and crescendo/diminuendo and ppp to fff dynamics processing. MIDI Meaning is reversible, i.e. if an accent is later removed the note in question will go back to its original length and velocity values; dynamics processing, however, brings about permanent changes to the MIDI data which cannot be reversed. When processing a score with MIDI Meaning or dynamics remember the importance of working on a *copy* to avoid confusion or loss of important material .

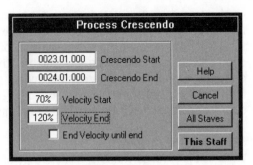

Figure 4.17. Programming a crescendo

That completes the treatment of the strings arrangement, which should resemble the same standard of presentation as that in Figure 4.14. Comparing the before and after scores of Figures 4.13 and 4.14 shows the enormous visual improvements which can be achieved using Score edit. If required, print the score, as described above.

◆ **TIP** ◆

To split chords of, for example, four notes onto four separate tracks to create four part arrangements, try using 'Explode' in Staff Functions. Select '3 new Tracks' and tick 'Lines to Track' and 'Bass to lowest voice'.

Project 3

Creating a lead sheet

This example is concerned with creating a Lead sheet comprised of chords, melody and lyrics. The order of events would usually be the input or editing of the melody line followed by the lyrics, which need the melody to latch onto, and lastly the chords, which could be created automatically from an existing chord track or entered manually.

A Lead sheet created in Score edit

Many readers will already have song arrangements containing the musical accompaniment alone. Some of the existing arrangement may be suitable in the creation of some elements of the Lead sheet but, very often, to achieve something presentable, the melody, and often the chords, will need to be entered into Cubase separately (manually or via MIDI), and the lyrics will always have to be added manually. The procedure for creating a lead sheet, as shown in Figure 4.18, is as follows:

Start with the melody
While in the Arrange window, make a copy of the melody Part(s) for the Lead sheet, select it and open Score edit. If a melody does not already exist then it will have to be recorded onto a new Track or the notes written manually in Score edit. The latter case might require the creation of a new empty Part of suitable length which could then be selected and worked upon in Score edit. Or the notes could be input in step-time.

Even if the melody already exists, it is often the case that, once the singer has worked on things and perhaps the lyrics have been updated, the melody as it originally existed is no longer accurate. This is certainly the case in the example where the melody started out as in Figure 4.19. Note that bars 15, 16 and 17 have been considerably updated in the final version (Figure 4.18). Updating the melody may involve moving the pitch or position of individual notes or changing the melodic content of entire passages. This kind of editing is best achieved in Score edit. Since we are aiming at a printable version of the Lead sheet start working in Page mode immediately.

Figure 4.19. The Lead sheet melody before editing

Set up Staff Settings and Global Settings
Use the information in the previous tutorials to set up the Staff Settings and Global Settings dialogues to achieve the correct key, bars across the page, display quantize and the overall initial look of the Layout. Use Auto Layout to format the page accordingly.

Add lyrics
Once the melody has been suitably corrected and the page layout is looking acceptable the lyrics can be added. Lyrics are entered using the 'Lyricx' symbol found in the Other symbols palette. Proceed as follows:

- Select the symbol and click on the melody note corresponding to the first word of the lyrics with the pencil tool (which will appear on the screen automatically). This opens a pop-up input box.
- Enter the first word or syllable but do not press return. Instead press the tab button which will automatically step to the next note in the melody, whereupon the next word or syllable of the lyrics may be entered into a new pop-up input box.
- Use the tilde symbol (~) between syllables; Cubase will use this to display correctly centred dashes between adjoining syllables.
- Press return after entering one line of lyrics, for example, in order to manage the results on the page. The freshly entered lyrics should already be clearly displayed in reverse video (blacked) attached to the corresponding melody. They may need to be re-aligned. As with other elements of the score, use the align functions in the Format menu to line up the lyrics (usually in a straight line under the corresponding staff).

In most respects the lyrics may be treated like any other type of text, including formatting the text font, size and style. However, if a note is moved the attached lyric is moved with it. In addition, when lyrics are first entered certain words may be grouped too closely together. This can usually be remedied using the Auto Layout button which will move both the notes and the lyrics to the appropriate spacings.

Tidy up the spacing
Despite the use of Auto Llayout to correct untidy spacings with the lyrics, some spacings may still be inappropriate. In these instances, notes may be graphically moved using the layout tool and, in so doing, the attached lyric will be moved with it. Simply select and drag the note. Movement is restricted to horizontal only, and changes in position will be entirely graphic with no effect on the MIDI data. Of course, the layout tool may also be used to move the note data for any other reason, to improve the graphic appearance and readability of the score.

Add the chords
The next task is to add the chords which, like the creation of the melody, may be achieved in a number of ways. The first and most obvious is simply to enter the chords manually using the chord symbol found in the Other symbols palette. The default chord symbol is shown as C 7/b9 and, when selected, the pencil tool appears on the screen as for the other symbols. Click on the staff at the appropriate bar and beat using the position indicator on the Status bar as a guide. This opens the Edit Chord Symbol dialogue (Figure 4.20), where the characteristics of the chord may be chosen as follows:

- The 'Root note' box selects the essential chord name.
- The chord name may subsequently be updated to minor, dominant 7th, major 7th etc. in the 'Type' menu.
- Any tension may be added by ticking the 'Tensions' boxes.

Figure 4.20. The Edit Chord
Symbol dialogue

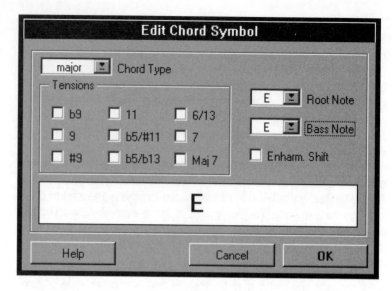

- Selecting 'Enharmonic shift' produces the flat version of the same chord i.e. : A# major becomes Bb major.
- An alternative bass note may be chosen from the 'Bass note' menu.
- Clicking on OK enters the chord symbol above the chosen bar and beat of the selected staff.

The actual style and appearance of the chord symbols may be further updated in the 'Chord font' section of the Global Settings dialogue. Here, the actual manner in which major 7th, minor, diminished and half diminished are displayed may be chosen, as well as the size of the symbols (Figure 4.21).

Figure 4.21(a). The Global
Setting Chord Font section

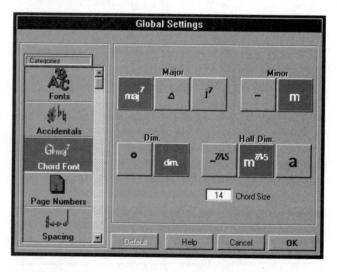

In addition to doing everything manually there is an alternative in the 'Do' menu called 'Make chords' (Atari/Falcon – Function menu). This feature automatically enters chord symbols onto the currently active staff. All notes on all staves are taken into consideration or the user may select specific groups of notes. There must be at least three notes at the same position in time for Cubase to interpret them as a chord. The user could use the chords from an existing Track or, if not available, a special chord Track could be quickly created. Both could be used to calculate the chord symbols.

It is always a good idea to heavily quantize chord tracks so that 'Make Chords' can interpret clearly where each chord is meant to be. The analysis produces inversions of chords when detected (a bass note is added to the symbol) but, if 'ctrl' is held while selecting Make Chords the essential chord name alone is entered. Make Chords is not always accurate and more complex chord shapes may need manual attention.

You may wish to include guitar style chord symbols on your scores. This is a purely graphic symbol, also found in the 'Other' symbols palette. Clicking with this symbol chosen enters a standard chord box representation of the six strings of the guitar onto the screen. Double clicking on the box opens the 'Edit guitar' dialogue.

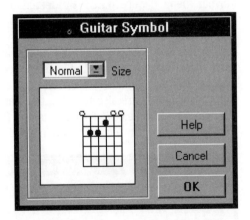

Figure 4.21(b). Edit Guitar symbol dialogue

Here, the size of the symbol, 'Regular' or 'Large', may be chosen and by clicking on the various fret positions of the strings, the fingering of any chord may be displayed.

By clicking outside of the box to the left of the first fret position, a fret number from 1 to 10 (in roman numerals I to X) may be added, and, by clicking at the top of any string, a O or X may be entered to denote that the string is either open or does not form part of the chord. These symbols are efficient and easy to use and look excellent on the score printout. Once the chord shape has been finalised the completed symbol may be dragged to the required position on the score.

The completed Lead sheet should resemble the same standard of presentation as that in Figure 4.18. If required, print out the score, as described above.

Having come this far, you should now have Score edit under control and be able to go on to explore most other aspects of the editor. However, before ending the Chapter, we need to look at one other important Score edit concept, the Layout layer.

The Layout Layer

Broadly speaking, a Layout is all those elements of a score which are not note specific. In other words, take away the notes and all things related to them and you are left with the Layout. The Layout Layer may be viewed by selecting 'Layout Layer Only'. However, the Layout does not include such things as the title, comment and copyright or page numbers, and Layouts are available only in page mode.

Each Layout consists of a specific group of Tracks which were chosen in the Arrange window. For example, if you selected trombone, saxophone and trumpet Tracks, worked on them in Score edit and then used 'Keep' to exit, a new Layout would be created. This Layout would be specific to these three Tracks and, if the same combination is reworked at a later stage, the previous Layout is overwritten if 'Keep' is used to exit. However, if the trumpet Track only is selected for editing in Score edit, then a new Layout would be created if 'Keep' is used to exit the editor.

A list of Layouts is found in the 'Page Mode Settings' dialogue of the Format menu (Figure 4.22). By default, Layouts are provisionally given the name of the first Track in each combination and these may be renamed by double clicking on the current name. The Layout currently residing in Score edit is indicated by a star and the Track combination used in each Layout is indicated in the Track list on the right. The display of Tracks is purely for reference and cannot be changed in any manner. The Layout names are also found in the main Edit menu in the 'Score layout' sub menu of 'Select'. This is excellent for finding the Track combination for different Score layouts within a complex arrangement.

Figure 4.22. Page Mode Settings dialogue

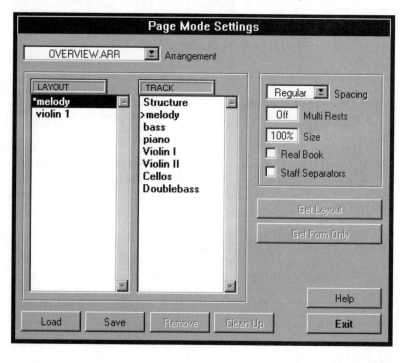

So, how can Layouts be useful? Theoretically, any Layout could be applied to any score but this would not usually be very constructive. One way of using Layouts is when a single instrument or group of instruments is extracted from a completed full score. By taking the Layout of the full score and imposing it upon the single instrument score, all rehearsal, repeat, segno, coda marks etc., along with various spacings and bar line settings, now appear on the single instrument staff.

To achieve this, with the single instrument Track in Score edit, simply select the Layout required, ('Full score', for example), from the Layout list in the 'Page Mode Settings' dialogue and select 'Get Layout' or 'Get Form Only'. The selected Layout will replace the current Layout. After using the 'Get' buttons, 'Keep' should be re-selected upon leaving Score edit in order to retain the new single instrument Layout. The new Layout can later be renamed and saved.

Different Layout elements are applied to the score according to which 'Get' button is selected, as in the following table:

INFO

Most versions of Cubase are supplied with a range of standard layouts, including popular brass, orchestral, keyboard and guitar configurations, which can be applied to your own scores as appropriate.

Get button selections

Layout elements	Button selected	
	Get layout	Get form only
Symbols from layout palette	all symbols	'rehearsal, segnos, codas and endings'
Bar line types	yes	yes
Bar number offsets	yes	yes
Staff settings dialogue values	all	None
Page mode dialogue values	all	None
Vertical spacing of staves	yes	no
Bar line spacing	yes	no
Staff spacing	yes	no
Broken bar lines	yes	no

Layouts are saved and loaded within the 'Page Mode Settings' dialogue and are given the file extension '.LAY'.

Final comment

That completes this practical introduction to Score edit. Expert users will realise that not absolutely all aspects of the editor have been covered. However, the aim of this chapter was to provide an easy and practical way into Score's secrets. Those aspects not covered tend to be the more esoteric and less used options and many readers will only ever need the essentials. In any case, armed with the practical information provided here, the user will feel confident to go on to explore any other aspects of Score edit.

Most readers will quickly establish their own way of working with Score edit and, of course, methods will vary according to each individual's needs. As with the other editors, there will be a tendency to become heavily reliant on the mouse, but remember that various keyboard commands and keyboard/mouse combinations can help in manipulating things quickly and easily. The following table outlines some useful smart moves for Score edit:

Smart moves for Score edit

Key	Mouse action	Result
alt + D	–	opens print dialogue
alt + B	–	hides selected item(s)
alt + E	–	opens enharmonic shift dialogue
alt + G	–	groups selected notes under one beam
alt + X	–	flips stems of selected notes
➡	–	selects next note
⬅	–	selects previous note
⬇	–	selects next staff
⬆	–	selects previous staff
keys 1 – 7	–	selects whole to 1/64 note values
T	–	selects triplet values
•	–	selects dotted note values
alt	click right mouse	moves song pos. pointer to mouse position
ctrl	click right mouse	opens current Symbols palette at mouse pos.
ctrl	input notes on staff with note tool	restricts notes to scale of chosen key sig.
alt	click on existing note with note tool	changes note length to current note value
alt	add note symbol from Symbols palette	adds symbol to all currently selected notes
shift	double click on note	selects all notes in current staff
ctrl	double click on note	selects all notes of same pitch from all staves
alt	double click on note	selects all octaves of same pitch from all staves
shift	double click on symbol	selects all symbols of the same kind
–	double click on almost any score item	opens dialogue box relevant to that item

5

Logical edit – the final frontier

Logical edit in theory

While it helps to have some knowledge of the theory of MIDI and basic mathematics, Logical edit is within the grasp of all users. It requires some initial effort but, once mastered, Logical edit provides some extremely fast methods of manipulating any kind of MIDI data. This chapter deals with the subject by practical example. Real situations likely to be met during the course of a typical Cubase session are outlined, as well as some of the more elaborate possibilities.

Before looking at Logical edit itself let's take some time to think about the logical aspects of music in general. Most users will already be aware that many aspects of music can be expressed as mathematical data. With MIDI, numbers are given to all the notes within the normal pitch range, numbers express the intensity (velocity) of these notes and MIDI based sequencers express their durations in terms of numbers of pulses (or ticks). So, if three of the fundamental elements of musical expression (pitch, velocity and duration) are being expressed as numbers then it should be an easy matter to carry out logical operations upon them.

Of course, there is no purely logical element in the making of good music but this is not the point of Logical edit. Logical edit is a tool which reduces certain kinds of otherwise extremely laborious edit operations to one or two clicks of the mouse.

You cannot, however, *see* any musical data in the Logical edit window, as you can in the other editors. Therefore, Logical edit could be regarded as a very elaborate, user changeable 'function', similar to those already found in the Functions menu but adaptable to each user's needs. It provides a facility with which custom designed processing tools can be assembled to fulfil a wide range of tasks.

Many potential Logical edit operations can be expressed in plain English. For example:

- 'IF the MIDI event type is a note THEN add ten to the velocity' or
- 'IF the MIDI event type is a note THEN fix the duration at 96' or
- 'IF the MIDI event type is a note and is equal to 36 THEN extract this note from the track and put it onto a new track'.

Here we will be exploring Logical edit in expert mode. Easy mode was considered to be just a little too easy for most users and lacked some of the more useful functions available in expert mode.

These statements are easy to understand and they describe actual Logical edit functions which are regularly used. If you can understand these statements then the next step is simply to translate their logic onto the Logical edit screen of Cubase.

The Logical edit window

Logical edit is opened from the Edit menu or by selecting ctrl + L from the computer keyboard (Figure 5.1). Note value (pitch), velocity and duration are found on the expert Logical edit screen as the Value 1, Value 2 and Length columns. These are clearly marked in the Filter and Processing sections. So we already know where to find some of the most important musical parameters on the Logical edit screen. It is now simply a matter of knowing how to manipulate them.

Why call the columns vague names like Value 1 and Value 2 ? This is because Logical edit can be made to act upon data other than notes, such as pitch bend and modulation, when the value columns assume different meanings. For the moment we are going to limit ourselves to note data alone.

The Filter and Processing sections may be regarded as equivalent to an IF, THEN statement as found in popular computer languages. Those already familiar with a computer language will understand the logic of this. Essentially the logic of the Logical edit screen can be simply expressed in the following statement:

Figure 5.1 The expert Logical edit screen

IF condition is true (or not true) THEN do the following calculation

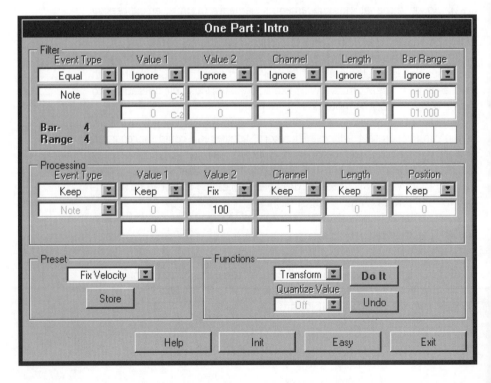

In the Filter section, one or a number of conditions are set which 'filter' the type of data going through and, in the Processing section, one or a number of calculations/actions are specified to take place on the data.

Opening the contents of the pop-up menus which are marked with downward pointing arrows reveals the myriad of possibilities available in Logical edit. However, things may have already become a little too complicated so let's get straight on to three introductory examples.

Logical solutions

Increasing the velocities of notes

Problem
The feel of the bass line you have just recorded is perfect but it was played too softly.

Solution
- While still on the Arrange window make sure the Part or Track in question is selected. Open Logical edit by selecting it from the Edit menu or use ctrl + L on the computer keyboard.
- Ensure that the screen is in expert mode and initialise it by clicking on the 'Init' button.
- Adjust the Filter section so that the Event Type (column 1) reads 'Equal Note'. Leave all other Filter columns in 'ignore' mode.
- Set the Processing section Value 2 column (velocity) to 'Plus 10'.
- If the screen has been correctly initialised Logical edit should already be in the default 'Transform' mode (see Figure 5.2).

Figure 5.2 Adding 10 to the velocity

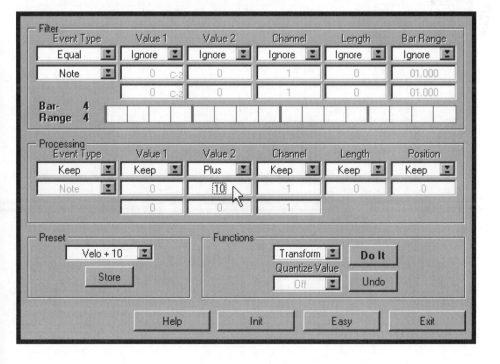

Clicking on 'Perform/Do It' adds 10 to the velocity of all notes in the chosen Part or Track thus making the result louder.

To verify the result try playing the Part while adding the velocity and click more than once if more velocity is required. Why 10 ? MIDI specifies a range of 0 – 127 for the velocity of notes and 10 makes a reasonable audible difference. But please note that not all synths react in the same way to velocity information and some are not velocity sensitive at all.

Making a part more staccato

Problem

You have recorded a repeating synth melody which is perfect except that you would like it to be more staccato. (i.e. notes with short durations).

Solution
- Select the Part or Track in question on the Arrange page and open Logical edit. Initialise the screen.
- Set the Filter section Event Type to 'Equal note'.
- Set the Processing section Length column to 'Fix 96'.
- Ensure that the Function mode is in 'Transform' (see Figure 5.3).

Clicking on 'Perform/Do It' will change the length of all notes in the chosen Part or Track to semiquavers i.e. short notes. Why 96 ? Cubase has a resolution of 384 pulses (ticks) per quarter note. There are four semiquavers in a quarter note. 384 divided by 4 equals 96. If this is not staccato enough then try 48 or even 24 in the Length column.

Figure 5.3 Setting all notes to short durations

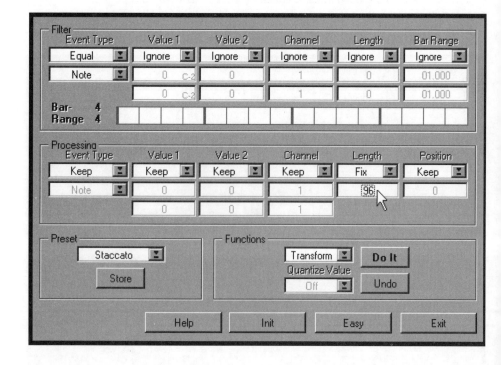

Separating the bass drum out to its own Track

Problem
You often program drums as MIDI tracks instead of Drum tracks and the Part you have recorded includes the bass drum, snare and hi-hat on the same Track. You would like to separate the bass drum onto its own Track in order to do some detailed editing.

Solution
- Open Logical edit from the Arrange window (since the Extract function is *not* available if you enter Logical edit from one of the editors).
- Set the Filter section Event Type column to 'Equal note', and the Value 1 column to 'Equal 36 (C1)'.
- Select 'Extract' in the Function mode pop-up menu.
- Leave all the columns in the Processing section in 'Keep' mode (see Figure 5.4).

Clicking on 'Perform/Do It' will extract note number 36 (or C1) from the Part and automatically create a new Track on the Arrange window within which to store the extracted notes.

Why note number 36 ? The range of the full piano keyboard is expressed in MIDI as note numbers 21 to 108. As many readers will already know, the standard position for the main bass drum happens to be 36. This is also usually the first key of the keyboard found on most modern synthesizers.

Figure 5.4 Extracting a bass drum

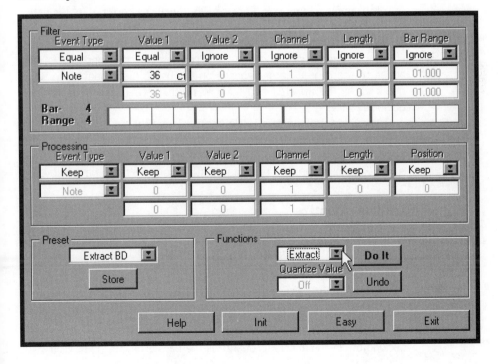

There are other ways of dealing with the above problems but these examples have been used as a simple way in to Logical edit. Things have been kept at a deliberately basic level to take into account those who have never used Logical edit before and those who maybe don't know too much about the theory of MIDI. Of course, Logical edit is capable of very much more elaborate and exciting functions.

Further exploration

The first example above considered increasing the velocity of *all* notes within the Part. This is not particularly subtle and the requirements of musicians are often a lot more elaborate than this. So how do we treat a Part where just a few notes are getting lost in the mix but the velocity level of the majority are OK. ?

It is simple really. A threshold is set below which the offending events alone will be subject to a set velocity increase. Or, in the language of Logical edit:

- Set the Filter section to 'Equal note' in the Event Type column and 'Lower (than) 30' (or some other threshold) in the Value 2 (Velocity) column.
- Set the Processing section Value 2 column to 'Plus 50' (or some other chosen level).
- Set the function to 'Transform'.

In this example, clicking on 'Perform/Do It' will search for all notes with a velocity (value 2) lower than 30 and add 50 to them. The result is that all previously inaudible notes will have been brought up to a reasonable level. Of course, the threshold set in the Processing section and the velocity added to the chosen notes depends on the user's judgement as to which notes should be affected and by how much. Each Part's treatment will obviously vary.

Things are becoming a little more elaborate but so far only the Transform and Extract functions have been used. However, there are also possibilities with quantize, delete, insert and copy, and, rather than use single columns to process the data, multiple columns could be employed.

Logical quantize

Imagine a composite drum Part where you wish to hard quantize just the bass drum leaving the feel of the rest of the kit intact. Simple:

- In the Processing section, select 'Equal note' in the Event Type column and specify the bass drum note in the Value 1 column.
- Select Quantize as the function and enter the required quantize value in the quantize pop-up menu.

Clicking on 'Perform'/'Do It' quantizes the bass drum to the desired value using Over quantize.

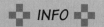

INFO

The main quantize functions of Cubase work upon note data alone but, using Logical edit, you may also quantize other kinds of data. This could be used, for example, to reduce pitch bend data. In the Processing section, simply select 'Equal pitch bend' in the Event Type column, choose a quantize value in the quantize pop-up and select the quantize function. This is a good alternative to 'Reduce continuous data' found in the main Functions menu which performs a similar thinning out of the data.

Logical delete

Users of GM compatible MIDI files are often delighted when all the program change messages embedded in the song call up the correct patches on their favourite GM modules and synths. However, many users will possess non-GM equipment and the program changes may wreak chaos when playing back the song. The simple answer is to delete them and put in your own program changes for each Track or Part.

There are several ways of deleting program changes but Logical edit probably provides the quickest:

- Select *all* Parts in the Arrangement using ctrl + A and open Logical edit using ctrl + L.
- In the Filter section, set the Event Type column to 'Equal program change'.
- Set 'Delete' in the functions pop-up menu.

Clicking on 'Perform/do It' deletes all program changes in the arrangement. This kind of operation could equally be applied to a single track or used to perform blanket deletions of other kinds of data. Remember, however, that program changes contained within the Inspector will not be included in the deletion process.

Logical insert

The Logical 'insert' function 'adds' notes to the Part or Track. For example, if you needed to double up the snare drum with a handclap in a drum part, Logical edit provides an easy way to do it:

- In the Filter section, select 'Equal note' in the Event Type column and the note of the snare drum in the Value 1 column.
- In the Processing section, select the note of the handclap in the Value 1 column.
- Select Insert as the function.

When used, the result is that for every snare drum that Logical edit finds in the Part or Track a handclap will be inserted at the same position. Using the other four columns of the Processing section the velocity, the MIDI channel, the length or the position of the handclap could also be changed.

Logical copy

'Copy' is similar to 'Extract' in that it is available only when entering Logical edit from the Arrange window. It is best used for situations requiring the selective copying of events onto a new Track. Simply set the Filter section Event Type, Value 1, and/or other, columns to the values of the data to be copied and select the 'Copy' function. A new Track will be automatically created in the Arrange window containing the copied data. Note that the Processing section is non-operational in 'copy' and 'extract' mode.

The processing possibilities

To get an idea of what else is available in Logical edit consider the wealth of functions available in the pop-up menus of the Processing section. There is the possibility of adding or subtracting, multiplying or dividing the chosen data by a given value, fixing the data type to a set value, setting a velocity ramp between two values, and random operations on data. Certain of these functions are better suited to specific data types and operations. For example:

- It is possible to raise the values of notes by one semitone using 'multiply by 1.02' ! but it is far easier to simply use 'plus 1'.
- The multiplication function is far better used in the Position column; if the position is multiplied by two this will halve the tempo of a given Part and if we divide by two this will double the tempo. These two functions are already saved as presets in the ten presets which come with Cubase.
- The dynamic function (dyn) can be effectively used in the Velocity column (Value 2) to produce crescendos and diminuendos. i.e. sequences can be faded in or out between two user defined values. This is effective for snare or timpani rolls and all other musical situations requiring dynamic ornamentation.
- It is probably irresistible to use the random function on note values at least once but random can be used to better effect with note velocity. If you have a Part that seems rather lifeless or a repetitive synth Part into which you wish to inject a little variation then entering, for example, a random variation between 85 and 100 in the Velocity column (Value 2) may be the answer.

A common problem in MIDI based music is the lifeless hi-hat, and this could be dealt with in a similar way to the previous example. However, introducing something a little more musical than randomness requires some Logical edit know-how and this leads us on to the next set of practical examples.

Hi-hat and rhythm processing

A lifeless hi-hat may be due to the choice of sound and/or the feel of the playing. The feel or the groove is dictated by the position and the accent of the notes. Position is better dealt with using Cubase's groove quantize, but accent can be processed very efficiently using Logical edit. A real drummer would obviously accent certain beats and these accents would also relate to what else is going on with the kit. It is almost impossible to recreate the feel of an excellent drummer but, using Logical edit, we can make up for some of the deficiencies of something that was badly played or input in step time.

This tutorial assumes that the hi-hat Part to be processed is very simple, i.e. continuous 1/16th notes occurring throughout a four bar pattern in 4/4 time. Only closed hi-hats are being taken into consideration. The

INFO

This section describes how to get some life back into an uninspired hi-hat part. This procedure could also be adapted for any kind of rhythmic material.

aim is to accent the first and third beats of each bar and to make all the down beats a little stronger than the up beats. Once the technique has been mastered in its basic form the user can go on to experiment with more elaborate procedures.

Select a hi-hat Part in the Arrange window that is in need of livening up and open Key edit, (or Drum edit if preferred). While in the editor select the Mastertrack list editor from the Edit menu. Double click in the 'Signature' column and change the time signature of the passage being processed to 4/16.

Why change the time signature? Because we need to prepare the scene for Logical edit to accentuate certain notes within each beat. 4/16 is equal to one quarter note beat in 4/4 time. This is a temporary change which will be reversed when processing is complete.

Now open Logical edit. Let's start by setting all the hi-hats to velocity values of between 70 and 80:

- Set the Filter section to 'Equal note' in the Event Type column.
- Set the Processing section to a random value of between 70 and 80 in the Value 2 column.
- Set Logical edit to 'Transform' and click on 'Perform/Do It' (see Figure 5.5).

Figure 5.5 Hi-hat variations

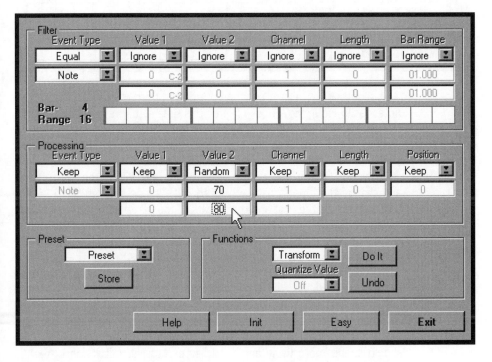

Each stage of the process can be saved as a preset for future use or some users may feel comfortable working on the fly. Presets are stored by holding 'alt' while selecting an existing preset which is to be overwritten. Clicking on 'Store' saves the current values under this preset name. Double clicking on the name opens an input box where a new name may be entered.

Next, a stress is required on all the down beats of the Part. A real drummer might do this but it depends on the style of the music. It is achieved in Logical edit by using the 'Bar Range' function of the Filter section. Without changing the previous Logical edit settings proceed as follows :

- Set a filter for all notes 'inside' the range '1.0 to 1.48' in the bar range column. This can be selected directly in the Bar Range column or the range can also be adjusted using click and drag in the graphic bar range found between the Filter and Processing sections.
- Set the Processing Value 2 column to plus 20 and click on the 'Perform/Do It' button (see Figure 5.6).

The graphic bar range is a graphic representation of a time segment of the music. With the current time signature set to 4/16 this time segment is equal to one beat. If the hi-hat Part contains continuous 1/16 notes then each successive group of four such notes will be acted upon according to how things are filtered.

Figure 5.6 Using bar range to target the down beats

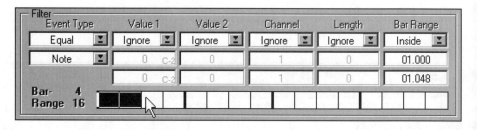

A slightly lesser accent could be put on the third of each group of 1/16 notes (as in Figure 5.7, above right), this time setting the Value 2 column to plus 10. The Bar Range filter should read 'inside 3.0 – 3.48'. Click on 'Perform/Do It' and play the hi-hat Part while still in Logical edit. Things should be sounding slightly more musical already.

Now exit Logical edit to get back to Key edit. Open the Mastertrack and change the time signature back to 4/4. Escape and return to Logical edit. Accents on the first and third beats of the bar will finish the exercise.

Figure 5.8 (below right) shows the accenting of the first beat of the bar, i.e. notes 'Inside 1.0 – 1.48' in the Bar Range column of the Filter section are processed with a 'plus 10' in the Value 2 (velocity) column of the Processing section. Finally the third beat of the bar is treated similarly but with a subtle velocity increase of 'plus 5'. As an alternative try accenting the second and fourth beats of the bar instead.

When you are satisfied with the results, go back into Key edit and 'keep' the changes to go back to the Arrange window. The hi-hat Part should sound more lively and musically expressive, but if more 'feel' is required then using one of the grooves in Groove quantize may be the answer.

If the results are not to your liking then you may need to experiment with the velocity values used in each preset. Not all hi-hats respond equally to velocity data, and subtle changes may not register at all in some

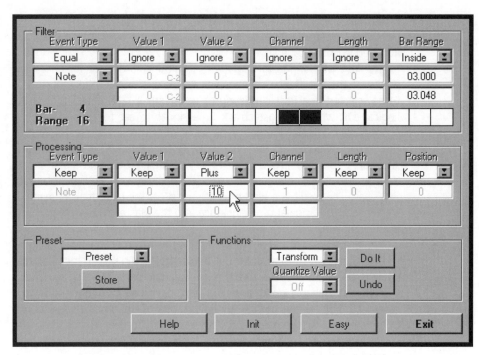

Figure 5.7 A slightly lesser accent

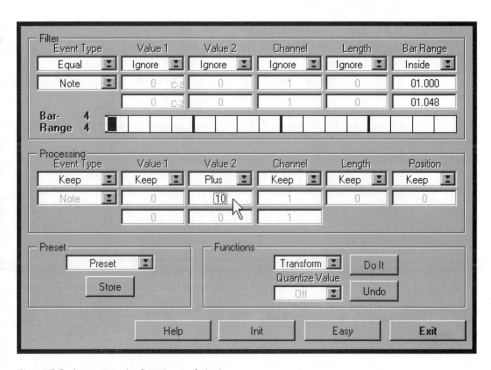

Figure 5.8 Accenting the first beat of the bar

drum machines. In order to achieve a satisfactory result, knowledge of how the target machine responds to velocity is as important as any knowledge of Logical edit.

The use of the Mastertrack with Logical edit greatly enhances the power of the Bar Range column. For example, if every other note needs to be selected in a Part consisting of equi-distant 1/16 notes, then using Logical edit with the Mastertrack time signature set to 2/16 makes the process easy. The Bar Range can be set to filter through either the first or the second of each pair of 1/16 notes. Experimentation with other time signatures can also prove fruitful. Try changing the time signature to 3/16 and then put an accent of 'plus 20' on the second 1/16 beat of each 3/16 bar. The result is a kind of continuous 'off the beat' feel. Remember to put back the original time signature into the Mastertrack after processing is complete.

The procedure for hi-hat parts described here can obviously be adapted to other kinds of musical data. But before going too wild remember that while it is easy to improve a very poor sounding part, it is also fairly easy to ruin a reasonably good sounding part. So tread carefully and always work with Logical edit out of Key Edit or one of the other edit windows. Only when you are completely satisfied should you keep the changes and go back to the Arrange window. This is particularly important if you have decided to process an entire Track.

Controlling the controllers

The so-called continuous controller type of MIDI data is a non-note part of the MIDI Specification used for controlling the notes themselves or other non-note parameters. Most readers will be familiar with pitch bend and modulation and the wheels that control them found on many synthesizers.

Pitch bend is not actually classed as a continuous controller but assumes its own special data type within the MIDI Specification. Modulation is usually classed as Controller number 1. These controllers could be processed in Logical edit but, it has to be said, that they are probably best left to the dedicated wheels and other parts of Cubase.

However, there are a number of more exotic controllers in the MIDI specification for which it is not always practical nor desirable to use the wheels. Logical edit can manipulate this kind of controller data in a way which would be difficult to achieve in real-time. In some instances, it is the only sensible method to achieve the desired result.

Imagine trying to record a fast, accurate MIDI auto-pan effect in real time; nearly impossible. But with Logical edit this kind of thing could be tackled reasonably quickly. What we need is a Logical edit controller tool-box. The examples outlined below show, above all, ways of 'inserting' controller events after the notes have been recorded. Let's start with auto-pan, but we will also be going on to explore tremolo and key gate effects, all created with the help of Logical edit.

Common to some of the tools will be the need to pre-fill the Part with a dummy controller. Why? Because when the 'Insert' function of Logical edit is used, the data to be inserted needs something to latch onto. 'Insert' adds new events to a Part only in relation to events already in existence in that Part. If a Part is empty 'insert' has no function. Hence, pre-filling the Part with dummy events ensures that new events can be added at the required resolution. All will become clearer as we go on.

Before going on to specific examples, let's just take a moment to understand some theory. When the Event Type is set to 'Control Change' in the Filter or Processing sections of the Logical edit window, the Value 1 and Value 2 columns assume different meanings. Instead of the MIDI note number, the Value 1 column corresponds to any one of the available controllers in the MIDI specification (modulation is specified as Controller number 1, volume is Controller number 7, pan is Controller number 10 and so on). Instead of velocity, the Value 2 column defines the setting of the chosen controller. Both columns may assume values of between 0 and 127.

Auto-pan

Now let's get down to business. To pre-fill the Part with dummy controller data proceed as follows:

• Choose or create a Part on the Arrange window and open List edit.
• Set the insert line to Control Change and set Snap to 8.
• Use 'fill' in the Function menu to insert dummy controller events at 1/8 note intervals. Leave the controller events at their default value of 0. Controller 0 should have no effect on the rest of your data but if it is not convenient, change it to one of the general purpose controllers between 16 and 19, for example, using Logical edit.
• 'Keep' the Part and then open Key edit.
• Open the Controller display and select the appropriate controller icon; a line of dummy controller events should be visible. These events should have no effect whatsoever on the actual music; they are simply used as the framework upon which we can attach other controller data which *will* have an effect on the music. The dummy events will be deleted after editing has been completed.

The auto-pan effect requires the creation of five Logical edit presets. These will be named as follows:

• pan L to R
• pan R to L
• select pan
• speed up
• slow down

The use of these presets requires the Part to have been filled with dummy controller events, as just described.

MIDI specifies Controller 10 as Pan. A value of 0 for this controller pans the sound to the extreme left and a value of 127 pans to the extreme right. The first preset, pan L to R, does simply that, it pans the chosen Track from left to right in the stereo image.

Inserting a ramp of left to right Pan events

To create the first preset proceed as follows:

- Open Logical edit in Expert mode.
- In the Filter section, set the Event Type to 'Equal control change' and the Value 1 column to 'Equal 0'.
- In the Processing section, 'Fix' the Value 1 column to 10, set the Value 2 column to a 'Dyn' setting of 0 to 127 and set the Position column to 'Divide' by 2.
- Set Logical edit to 'Insert' mode and store as a preset under the appropriate name (see Figure 5.9).

This preset inserts an ascending ramp of Controller 10 events for every dummy controller event it finds.

Figure 5.9 Inserting a ramp of left to right pan events

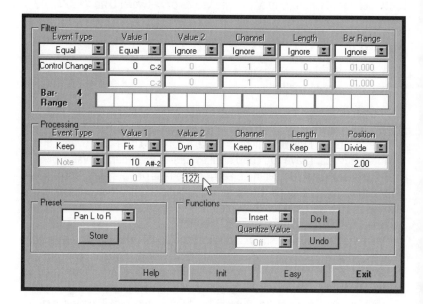

Inserting a ramp of right to left Pan events

For the second preset, pan R to L, proceed as follows:

- In the Filter section, set the Event Type to Control Change and the Value 1 column to 'Equal 10'.
- In the Processing section, 'Fix' the Value 1 column to 10, set the Value 2 column to 'Invert' and set the Position column to 'Plus' 768.
- Once again, set Logical edit to 'Insert' mode and store as a preset under the appropriate name (see Figure 5.10).

This preset will use the controller data created by the first preset to insert an inverted version of the events half a bar (768 ticks) later.

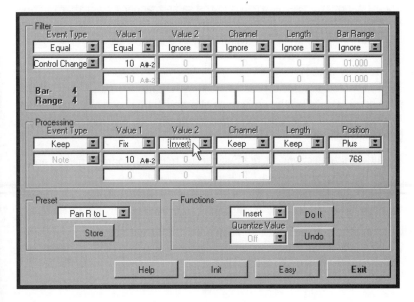

Figure 5.10 Inserting a Right to Left Pan

Select Pan

For the Select pan preset proceed as follows:

- In the Filter section, set the Event Type to 'Equal control change' and the Value 1 column to 'Equal 10'.
- Ignore the Processing section, set Logical edit to 'Select' mode and store as a preset (see Figure 5.11).

This preset simply selects all Pan data in the Part. Note that the Select function is available only if Logical edit has been opened from one of the other editors.

Figure 5.11 Selecting Pan data

Speed up preset

For the speed up preset proceed as follows:

- In the Filter section, set the Event Type to 'Equal control change' and the Value 1 column to 'Equal 10'.
- In the Processing section, set the Position column to 'Divide' by 2.
- Set Logical edit to 'Transform' mode and store as a preset (see Figure 5.12).

Figure 5.12 The speed up preset

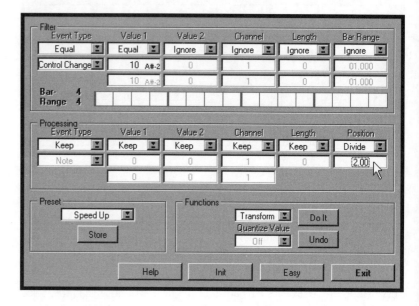

Slow down preset

The slow down preset is created in the same manner except that multiply by 2 should be entered in the Position column. The speed presets double or halve the speed of all Pan events they find in the Part.

DelDummy preset

Finally, before using the presets we must create one more general purpose preset which will be used to delete the dummy controller data initially recorded into the Part. We will name this as DelDummy and it is created as follows:

- In the Filter section, set the Event Type to 'Equal control change' and set the Value 1 column to 'Equal 0'.
- Ignore the Processing section.
- Set Logical edit to 'Delete' mode and store as a preset.

Of course, this preset must be adapted if a different number dummy controller has been used.

Using auto-pan tools

That completes the creation of the auto-pan tools. To use them, proceed as follows:

- Create a new two bar Part on the Arrange window and fill it with dummy controller events as described above.
- Set the Track of the new Part to the appropriate MIDI channel i.e. the same MIDI channel as the Track to which you wish to apply an auto-pan effect.
- Select the new Part and open Key edit. Select the Pan Controller from the menu in the Controller display by clicking on the controller icon.
- Set a one bar loop by clicking and dragging the mouse pointer in the position bar. Make sure that the pop-up event 'Select' menu, (next to the Goto menu), is in looped mode.
- Action the first auto-pan preset, Pan L to R, from the pop-up logical presets menu found in the main Functions menu. A number of Pan events will be inserted into the first half of the selected bar.
- Go back to the logical presets menu and action the second preset Pan R to L. This takes care of the second half of the bar with an inverted copy of the first half.

The first two presets have been designed to work with a looped 1 bar section in 4/4 time. You should now have a 'pyramid' shaped pattern of Pan events visible in the controller display (Figure 5.13).

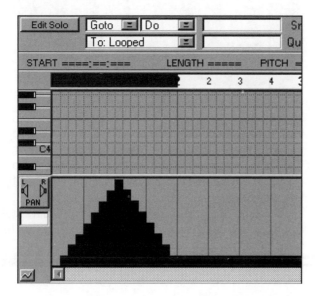

Figure 5.13 The pan pyramid

This pyramid is the essential building block of the auto-pan. At the moment it will smoothly pan a sound from left to right and back to left again over a length of one bar. What is needed now is a way of repeating the pan over the length of the Part and of managing the speed of the auto-pan. This is achieved with a combination of the Logical edit auto-pan tools and other functions of Cubase as follows:

108   *Fast Guide to Cubase*

- First, select all Pan events using the 'Select pan' preset.
- If you have created a Part of four bars or more, make sure that the pop-up edit 'select' menu is in 'Selected looped' mode and use 'Repeat' found in the pop-up 'Function' menu of Key edit. The selected looped section, (i.e. the Pan events alone), will be repeated up to the end of the part.
- If you have created a two bar Part, as recommended, it is easier to use the copy and paste functions found in the Edit menu to repeat the data.
- To change the speed of the auto-pan, de-select the loop and use the speed up and slow down presets.
- Continue to use Key edit's 'repeat', or 'copy and paste', with the Logical edit speed presets to arrive at the desired result. Very fast, perfectly formed auto-panning is possible (see Figure 5.14).

Figure 5.14 The Final Result

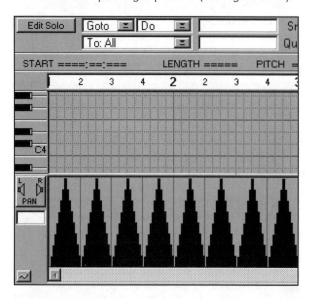

TIP

This kind of effect is pushing a lot of data all at once down that poor old MIDI cable, so, if possible, separate things to different MIDI outputs. As with all effects, beware of the tendency to over use.

This kind of effect is difficult to achieve without the Logical edit auto-pan toolbox. Finally, when completely satisfied with the result use the 'DelDummy' preset, as described above, to delete all the dummy controller events that were input at the beginning of the operation and leave Key edit using 'keep'.

Remember that a very long Part full of pan data should not be created as this quickly becomes very memory hungry. A two bar Part is usually sufficient. Once back on the Arrange page, ghost parts of the original can be created and the auto-pan repeated for as long as desired.

Tremolo

The creation of Logical edit presets to create a MIDI tremolo effect is really very easy since the presets required are almost exactly the same as the auto-pan presets.

Tremolo is the rapid variation of the volume of a signal at a fixed rate and depth – the rate and depth are usually adjustable to produce the desired intensity and effect. So, to create this effect with MIDI, we will need to manipulate Controller 7 (Volume) data.

Proceed as follows:

- Load in or create the auto-pan presets (if they are not already in memory) as described above, and go into Logical edit.
- Every time you see a 10 (Pan) in the Value 1 column of either the Filter or the Processing sections of each preset, change this to a 7 (Volume).
- Store the new settings under new preset names and then follow the procedure for use as described for the auto-pan operation.
- This time you will be working on Volume data and not Pan data so you will need to be looking at Volume data in the Controller display of Key edit.
- Remember that, in order for things to work properly, you must prefill the Part with dummy Controller 0 events (or another dummy controller number if 0 is not suitable).

Alternatively, take an existing Part containing auto-pan data and simply convert the Pan data to Volume data using Logical edit. Remember, however, that the rate of the tremolo effect will invariably be faster than that of an auto-pan. The result, in both cases, is a very convincing and effective tremolo effect (Figure 5.15).

✦ *INFO* ✦

You may have found the creation of the auto-pan and tremolo presets involved an inordinate amount of work, but remember that, once created, they can be saved to disk as part of a 'Set-up' or 'Song' file.

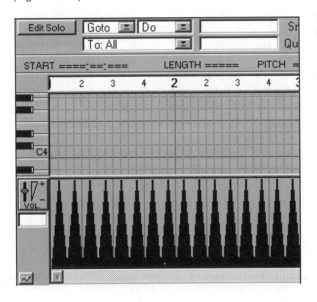

Figure 5.15 A MIDI tremolo effect

Key-trigger gate

The final tools for the Logical edit Controller toolbox simulate a key-trigger gate effect. The process involves the manipulation of Volume data but before creating the necessary presets we must first understand what is meant by a key-trigger gate effect.

Most readers will know what a noise gate is; it is an audio device which opens or closes the signal path according to various threshold and rate settings found on the unit. Among its simplest functions might be to close the signal path at a low threshold setting in order to block out unwanted background noise (in between the sung lines of a vocalist, for example). The signal path from the microphone would only be open when the vocalist is actually singing. Thus the opening and closing of the gate responds according to the characteristics of the input signal in relation to the user settings on the unit.

However, the gate can also be set to respond to a secondary input source. This is usually known as the key input. In this mode, for example, a sustained chord sound (Main signal) could be gated in and out according to the rhythm of a hi-hat (Key Input signal).

A simple key-trigger effect can be mimicked using MIDI Volume data. The aim of the exercise would be to control the volume level of one Track according to the rhythm and intensity of another. The notes and the velocities of the chosen key source Track would be translated into Volume data. When there *is* a note the MIDI gate would be open and when there is *not* a note it would be closed.

With Logical edit it is easy to translate notes into Volume Controller events. The note values themselves need not be translated. Each note event can be simply fixed as a Controller 7 (Volume) event in the Value 1 column of Logical edit. The velocities of the notes in the Value 2 column can be directly translated into the actual Volume level for each Controller 7 event.

So the opening of the MIDI gate presents no real problem but the closing of the gate is not so simple. Logical edit does not allow access to the Note Off element of note events. It is, therefore, not possible to use the end of a note as the point in time to close the gate, by inserting a zero Volume event. The solution involves the creation of four Logical edit presets which will become part of our ever expanding Logical edit controller toolbox. They are named, in the order in which they will be used, as KeyGate 1, 2, 3 and 4.

For the purposes of this exercise, reference will be made to 'zero volume' and 'volume up' events. Zero volume refers to MIDI Controller 7 events with their levels set to 0, and volume up refers to MIDI Controller 7 events with their levels set to anything between 1 and 127.

Creating KeyGate 1

KeyGate 1' involves the insertion of zero volume events and is created in Logical edit in expert mode as follows:

- In the Filter section, set the Event Type to 'Equal note' and the Length column to 'Lower than 144'.
- In the Processing section, 'Fix' the Event Type to 'Control Change', 'Fix' the Value 1 column to 7, 'Fix' the Value 2 column to 0 and the Position column to 'Plus 40'.
- Set Logical edit to insert mode and store as a preset under the appropriate name (see Figure 5.16).

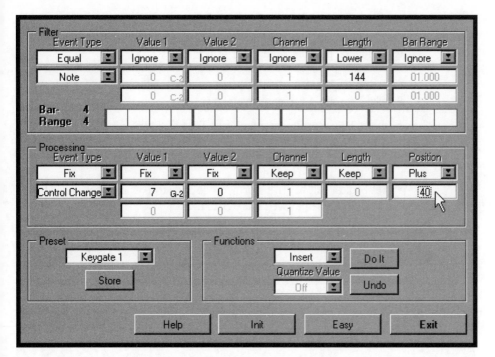

This preset inserts zero volume events at just under 1/32 (40 ticks) of a
note after the onset of each note it finds within the Part whose length is
less than a dotted 1/16 note (144 ticks). Or to put it more simply, this
preset produces the closing of the gate at a very short period after the
onset of each very short note it finds in the Part.

Figure 5.16 KeyGate 1

Creating KeyGate 2

The Logical edit settings for KeyGate 2 are similar to KeyGate 1 except
that the Length column of the Filter section should be changed to 'Inside
144 – 240' and the Position column of the Processing section should be
changed to 'Plus 88'.

This preset works in the same way as KeyGate 1 but is concerned with
notes of slightly longer duration.

Creating KeyGate 3

KeyGate 3 is, once again, similar to the first two presets except that the
Length column of the Filter section should be changed to 'Higher than
239' and the Position column of the Processing section should be changed
to 'Plus 136'. This preset inserts zero volume events for all the remaining
longer notes within the Part.

You may be asking why three presets have been created when one
would have been sufficient. It's true that we could have regulated the
length of the gate with one simple preset but an attempt has been made
to create something a little more musical which, after exhaustive tests,
was found to simulate more closely the actions of a real key-trigger gate
effect. In any case, those readers requiring something very simple could

use a single preset for the purposes of the zero volume Part of this exercise and, of course, the settings of each preset could be changed for experimental purposes and other effects.

Creating KeyGate 4

Finally, KeyGate 4 is created as follows:

- In the Filter section, set the Event Type to 'Equal note' and ignore all other columns.
- In the Processing section, 'Fix' the Event Type to 'Control Change' and 'Fix' the Value 1 column to 7.
- Set Logical edit to 'Transform' mode and store as a preset under the appropriate name (see Figure 5.17).

Figure 5.17 KeyGate 4

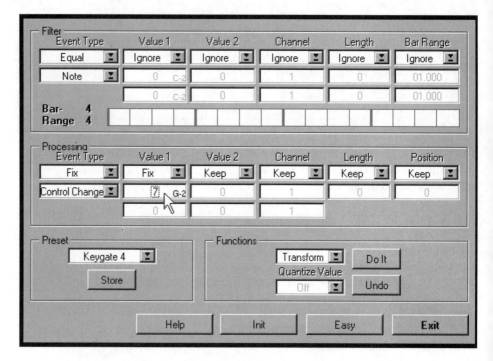

This preset is the volume up part of the procedure. It transforms all notes in the Part into volume up events. At the same time, the velocities (Value 2) of these notes are transformed into the actual volume level for each event. In this way, not only do we have a key-trigger gate effect which is sensitive to the length of the notes (thanks to the first three presets) but we have one which is also sensitive to the intensity (velocity) of the playing.

Using the Keygates

To use the presets proceed as follows:

- Copy the Part, or mix down the Parts, that you wish to use as the source for the key-trigger gate effect. A hi-hat Part or a bass drum and snare are good for testing the effect.

- Select the new Part and open Key edit.
- Select Volume in the Controller display and use the four Logical edit presets in their numbered order from the pop-up logical presets menu found in the main Functions menu.

The first three presets insert zero volume events so there will be no changes particularly visible in the Controller display window, but the moment KeyGate 4 is used all notes in the Part will disappear and be replaced by a corresponding series of Volume events. Figure 5.18 shows two Key edit windows displaying the original Part at the top, and the same Part, after processing, below it.

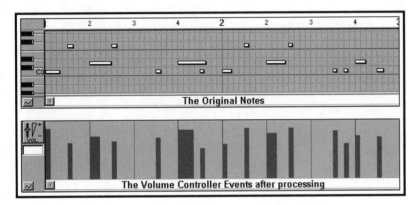

Figure 5.18 Before and after using the KeyGate tools

When you are satisfied with the results, use 'Keep' to go back to the Arrange window. Change the KeyGate Track to the desired MIDI channel and the Volume data will be imposed upon any music already on that channel. Alternatively, try playing a sustained chord on the chosen channel while cycling on the KeyGate Part.

The settings of the presets were established after tests with various rhythm patterns and, if the source Parts are well chosen, there should be no problems. The KeyGate presets may be saved as part of a Set up or Song file and loaded back into Cubase when required.

That completes the beginnings of the Logical edit Controller toolbox. Additional tools for some of the other controllers in the MIDI specification could be created in a similar fashion and the techniques mastered here could be used to control other kinds of MIDI data.

Logical conclusion

The examples presented here provide a useful companion to the Logical edit section of the Cubase manual, and those readers who re-created these examples for themselves will have benefited most.

Logical edit is best understood in the actual doing rather than in the theory. It is hoped that this chapter has helped de-mystify Logical edit and that you will be encouraged to explore the Logical edit window further.

Knowing Logical edit can lead to a more complete understanding of

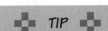

✦ *TIP* ✦

Remember that, once created, the presets can equally be actioned while remaining in the Arrange window. The process is not particularly memory hungry so even an entire Track can be processed. Just remember to copy the Part or the Track before editing as all note data will be irretrievably transformed.

MIDI and Cubase itself. By combining the strengths of different parts of the program with the power of Logical edit, the user is encouraged to understand the real capabilities of the whole system. And, if Logical edit has been mastered, then Cubase's 'Input Transform' function in the Options menu becomes child's play.

Lastly, as a general rule to using Logical edit, always initialise the screen before setting up an edit or changing Presets. Also remember that, if Logical edit is opened from one of the other editors after having selected a note, the Filter section will display the note value and velocity of that selection. This increases the speed with which users can target specific data for Logical edit processing.

Final recommendations

This book provides Cubase users with the essential tools of the trade, but exactly how creatively these tools are used is up to each individual. It must be appreciated that the tools themselves do not actually create the music. There is no artificial replacement for musicians, composers and arrangers, and Cubase does not pretend to be a substitute for musical talent. It does, however, facilitate the creation of great music when in the hands of the right programmer and when a reasonable musician or composer is providing the musical input. Cubase can also help you to learn more about music in general and can provide fresh approaches to the creative process.

You will find your own preferred methods of working with Cubase, but almost everyone will fall victim to bad habits and poor preparation at some time in their use of the system. To avoid some of the minor pitfalls it is often sufficient simply to be aware of them and correct the problems as they occur. These might include repetitive habits which slow down and impede your overall operational efficiency. Slightly larger problems might occur when you have not streamlined the program for optimum performance with your own system, or when you have limited knowledge of the hardware in use. The following points might help identify some of the common problem areas.

Keyboard shortcuts
Knowledge of the keyboard shortcuts can significantly increase your operational efficiency. If you find yourself totally reliant on the mouse, you should perhaps review your approach. A good mix of both mouse and keyboard moves would seem to be best.

Working with editors
If you find yourself disorientated when working in the editors, try the following: before opening an editor, position the left and right locators at the start and end points of the chosen Part using alt + ctrl + P, (or alt + P in the Atari/Falcon version). Also select cycle on the transport bar. This helps you navigate around the chosen Part and avoids the song position pointer disappearing from view.

Ctrl + E will open Key edit (or another default editor), for the chosen Part but, in many circumstances, it might be easier to simply double click on the Part, which will also open the editor.

After working in an editor and wishing to leave without keeping the edits, it is often easier to use the escape key (Esc), rather than search to close the window using the mouse. Similarly, if keeping the edits, it is often easier to use the Return key. It soon becomes apparent that some tasks are faster using the mouse and others using a keyboard shortcut. Remember also that the Esc and Return keys have similar actions when leaving all windows and dialogues.

Once in an editor you might feel the need to manipulate the notes using only the mouse. This can be clumsy when, for example, stepping through a sequence of notes in a melody. In this case, it is more efficient to use the left and right arrows of the computer keyboard. In addition, by selecting the loudspeaker (Mac and PC) or ear (Atar/Falcon) symbol in the Functions bar, you can monitor each note as it is selected.

When you find yourself indulging in editing tasks which seem laboriously repetitive and time consuming, remember Logical edit. This editor can often provide a solution which will save a lot of time and energy.

Don't overdo the quantizing

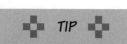

It is often better to try several takes to achieve a good musical performance rather than to attempt the correction of a poor one.

A tendency to over use the quantize functions is a common pitfall with most sequencer users, sometimes resulting in music which is robotic and lifeless.

Using quantize as the magic cure for all musical evils should be avoided. If quantize really has to be used then try Iterative quantize first as this will tighten up the feel of the performance without destroying the original inspiration.

However, some styles of music actually rely on hard quantize and strictly regulated grooves, so deciding when and how to use the quantize functions must be judged separately for each musical situation.

Customise Cubase

Many users continue to use Cubase with the windows sized and positioned in their default configurations. Remember that the Arrange window and editors can be sized and positioned according to your needs and saved as part of a definition file.

Some users also continue to use the system with many other aspects of the program left in their default positions. By customising the program in relation to the rest of the hardware in the MIDI system and the kinds of settings, modules and preferences required, many of the small obstacles which may impede the overall smooth operation of the software are eliminated. Don't shy away from taking some time to set up your own customised version of the system and saving this as a definition file.

Know your system

You may sometimes encounter operational problems owing to a lack of experience with your computer platform. You should try to be proficient in all aspects of your chosen platform and operating system as this can only help in your understanding of Cubase.

Knowledge of the hardware connected to Cubase, including the keyboards, modules and interfaces which go to make up a MIDI network, is often lacking too. It's well worth learning all you can about the units in your system. Some knowledge of MIDI will also help in the operation of the program and in solving any problems which may occur.

And finally ...
I hope you have found this book useful in your quest for an understanding of Cubase. Equipped with the essentials provided here you should feel confident to go on to explore other aspects of the program.

As final words of advice, remember that the aim of the exercise is to create music, let your ears be the final judge, take plenty of breaks from being glued in front of that computer screen and, most of all, enjoy it !

Glossary

Active Sensing A MIDI message sent by a master MIDI instrument to a slave to guard against MIDI errors such as notes which drone on endlessly because they have not received a Note Off message. If Active Sensing messages stop being sent, the slave assumes that there has been some kind of system error and immediately returns to its power up state, switching all droning notes off.

Active Sensing was designed primarily to mute MIDI modules if they lose contact with a remote keyboard. Most sequencers do not record or transmit this kind of data. It is not implemented by all manufacturers and is not an essential requirement for all MIDI devices.

Aftertouch The action of applying pressure to one or more keys of the musical keyboard after the onset of a note or chord. It is transmitted via MIDI as Aftertouch messages and is also referred to as 'Channel Aftertouch' or 'Channel Pressure' and affects all notes present on the same MIDI channel by the same amount. It can be used to produce various performance effects by changing, for example, the volume, vibrato or brightness of a sound. Aftertouch is not implemented on all instruments.

Balance MIDI controller number 8. Used to adjust the balance in volume between two components of a sound.

Bank Select A combination of MIDI Controller numbers 0 and 32. A Bank Select message allows switching to as many as 16384 different banks and is usually immediately followed by a program change.

Breath Controller MIDI Controller number 2. Used to change the volume or timbre of a sound via MIDI using a breath controller connected to a synthesizer.

Bit Binary digit. The smallest unit of digital information, represented as a 1 or a 0 in binary numbers.

Byte An 8 bit unit (an 8 bit binary number e.g. 0011 1010), creating the fundamental unit of measurement for computer media.

Control Change In MIDI based music, Control Change messages are used to control various parameters other than the notes themselves. Control Change messages are also known as MIDI controllers or continuous controllers. They provide a more generalised kind of MIDI message which can be used to control a wide variety of functions. Control Change messages contain information about the Controller number (0 – 127) and its value (0 – 127). Each controller number has a specific function and the more commonly used controllers are as follows:

Controller 01 – Modulation
Controller 02 – Breath Controller
Controller 07 – Main Volume
Controller 10 – Pan
Controller 11 – Expression
Controller 64 – Sustain Pedal

Controllers 32 – 63 provide the LSB (least significant bit) for Controllers 0 – 31. Control change messages are also used to transmit 'Reset All Controllers' messages (Controller 121), 'Local On/Off' messages (Controller 122) and MIDI Mode changes to devices (Controllers 124 – 127).

EBU   Acronym for 'European Broadcasting Union', an organisation responsible for setting audio and broadcasting standards in Europe.

Expression   MIDI Controller number 11. Used to change the volume of a note while it is sustaining.

General MIDI (GM)   An addition to the MIDI protocol (not formally a part of the MIDI Specification) providing a standard set of rules for patch mapping, drum and percussion note mapping, multi-timbrality, polyphony and various other elements. MIDI devices supporting this standard are known as GM or GM compatible instruments. Theoretically, music recorded using one GM module should be compatible with the parameters and sounds of any other. The essential requirements for GM instruments are as follows:

• It must provide a standard bank of 128 pre-defined sound types organised according to a standard patch map. For example, programs 1 – 6 are specified as various kinds of piano, program 7 is a harpsichord, 8 is a clavinet and so on.
• It must support all 16 MIDI channels and provide 16 part multi-timbrality if required.
• It must provide 24 note dynamically allocated polyphony or 16 note dynamically allocated polyphony with 8 voices reserved for drums and/or percussion.
• drum and percussion sounds must be on MIDI Channel 10 and mapped in accordance with standard GM positions.
• A GM Instrument must also provide the ability to respond to Pitch Bend, Modulation, Main Volume, Pan, Expression, Sustain, Reset all Controllers, All Notes Off, Aftertouch, Registered Parameters for Pitch Bend sensitivity and master tuning and Universal System Exclusive messages for switching GM Mode on and off.

The Roland Corporation have introduced an enhanced version of the GM standard known as GS and Yamaha have introduced similar enhancements known as XG. Hence, some MIDI devices now appear with the statement GM/GS compatible or GM/XG compatible.

Hexadecimal A base sixteen numbering system often used by computer programmers as an alternative to decimal or binary systems. The decimal numbers 0 – 9 are expressed as 0 – 9 in hexadecimal and decimal 10 – 15 are expressed as the letters A – F. Various symbols are used to denote that a number is hexadecimal including H or $ signs.

The hexadecimal number 09H (zero – nine) = 9 (nine) in decimal, 0AH (zero – A) = 10 (ten), 0BH = 11, 10H = 16, 15H = 21, 1AH = 26 and FFH = 255.

Hexadecimal numbers have much more in common with the way that computers actually work than decimal numbers and they are less cumbersome than binary numbers. Thus they have proved extremely efficient for the analysis and understanding of computer data.

Main Volume See Volume.

Master Keyboard Strictly speaking, a master keyboard is a MIDI equipped keyboard with no sound generating circuitry used to control a MIDI network of sound generating modules and devices. However, the term is also commonly used to refer to any electronic keyboard instrument which is used as the main keyboard in a MIDI network, whether it has sound capabilities or not. The keyboard at the centre of a MIDI network is also sometimes referred to as the 'mother keyboard'.

MIDI Acronym for Musical Instrument Digital Interface. A data communication standard, first established in 1983, for the exchange of musical information between electronic musical instruments and, subsequently, computers. This involves the serial transfer of digital information, (MIDI messages), via 5 pin DIN connectors. Like any other language or code, these messages are governed by a pre-defined set of rules and syntax. MIDI's set of rules is known as the MIDI Specification.

MIDI Channel MIDI devices send and receive data on 16 MIDI channels through a single cable. Most MIDI messages which make up this data are encoded with one of these channel numbers. Each MIDI device can be set to be receptive to messages on one of these channels or, in the case of a multi-timbral instrument, on several specified channels at the same time. This allows the sending of data to specific instruments or sounds within the same MIDI network. Many instruments can also be set to receive on all MIDI channels at the same time (Omni On mode).

MIDI Clock (MIDI timing clock) A timing related MIDI message embedded in the MIDI data stream. MIDI Timing Clocks are sent 24 times per quarter note and along with 'Song Position Pointer', 'Start', 'Stop' and 'Continue' messages are used to synchronize MIDI based sequencers, drum machines and other MIDI devices. Unlike SMPTE/EBU Time Code, MIDI Timing Clock is tempo-dependent.

MIDI Controller A type of MIDI message used to control various musical parameters other than the notes themselves, such as Modulation, Volume and Pan. Controllers are also referred to as 'Continuous Controllers' and 'Control Change messages'. This kind of data is often manipulated using the wheels and other physical controls found on MIDI equipped keyboard instruments (see Control Change for full details).

MIDI Event Used to refer to any MIDI data once it has been recorded into a MIDI based sequencer. This is in contrast to 'MIDI message' which refers to the same data as it is being sent down the MIDI cable.

MIDI File Also referred to as Standard MIDI Files, provide a way of transferring MIDI data between different software sequencers, hardware sequencers and computer platforms. There are three kinds of Standard MIDI File known as Type 0, Type 1 and Type 2. Type 0 stores the data as a single stream of events, Type 1 files contain multiple parallel tracks and Type 2 allows sets of independent sequences to be stored in a single file. Type 0 Files are the simplest and most portable but Type 1 files tend to be the most popular and convenient format with computer based sequencers.

MIDI Interface Refers to a hardware interface which provides a link between, for example, a computer and external MIDI devices. A MIDI interface normally provides at least one MIDI input and one MIDI output, and more advanced units provide multiple MIDI sockets and synchronization facilities. MIDI Interfaces may plug into the serial or parallel ports of the host computer or, in the case of the PC, may be in the form of a card which is installed inside the computer. The Atari ST and Falcon range of computers feature a built in MIDI Interface.

MIDI In 5 pin DIN socket found on all MIDI equipped instruments used to receive MIDI data. The receiving instrument might receive data from a variety of sources including a master keyboard or a sequencer.

MIDI Out 5 pin DIN socket found on all MIDI equipped instruments used to send MIDI data. When played, a master keyboard would send out Note On and Note Off messages via its MIDI Out.

MIDI Thru 5 pin DIN socket found on most MIDI equipped instruments providing a copy of the MIDI data received at the MIDI In. In other words, the data passes *through* the unit on to a further destination, such as another module. Some early MIDI instruments did not provide a MIDI Thru socket.

MIDI Machine Control (MMC) A more recent addition to the MIDI Specification to facilitate the control of tape transports and other devices. The code has a standard protocol which, when more devices adopt it, will facilitate the remote control of machines via MIDI.

MIDI Message The data transferred between MIDI equipped instruments contains MIDI Messages. MIDI messages include such things as Note on, Note Off, Polyphonic Pressure, Control Change, Program Change, Aftertouch, and System Exclusive data.

For example, when a key is pressed on a MIDI keyboard this sends out a Note On message via MIDI. The first part of this message specifies its message type, known as the Status Byte, and the second part of the message contains two elements expressing the pitch (or note number) and the velocity (the strength or speed) of the event, known as the Data Bytes. When the key is released a Note Off MIDI message is sent out via MIDI.

This contains a different Status Byte followed, once again, by two data bytes describing the pitch of the note and the speed with which it was released. Any MIDI instrument set to receive this data would understand the messages and instruct the sound making part of its circuitry to play a note of the appropriate duration, pitch and velocity.

MIDI Mode In addition to the rules governing the actual language of MIDI there are also four MIDI modes which govern how a receiving device reacts to data on different MIDI channels and whether it will perform polyphonically or monophonically. These modes are defined as follows:

Mode 1 – Omni On/Poly. The receiver responds to data on all MIDI channels and performs polyphonically.
Mode 2 – Omni On/Mono. The receiver responds to data on all MIDI channels and performs monophonically.
Mode 3 – Omni Off/Poly. The receiver responds only to data sent on its chosen MIDI Channel(s) and performs polyphonically.
Mode 4 – Omni Off/Mono. The receiver responds only to data sent on its chosen MIDI channel(s) and performs monophonically.

Most electronic keyboard instruments and modules power up in Mode 3 which is appropriate for most applications. Mode 4 is an advantage for MIDI guitar users where six monophonic MIDI channels can be selected to respond to the six strings of the guitar, each with its own separate note allocation and pitch bend. This mirrors more exactly the actual performance characteristics of a guitar.

MIDI devices may not always include all the MIDI modes in their specification.

MIDI Module A sound generating device with no integral keyboard. MIDI modules are most often standard 19 inch rackmount units which can be neatly arranged in any rackmount system in the studio or at home.

MIDI Time Code (MTC) A type of time code which can be sent via MIDI, used to synchronize MIDI based sequencers and other MIDI devices. Similar to SMPTE/EBU time code, MTC is an absolute timing reference measured in hours, minutes, seconds and fractions of a second and so does not vary with tempo. MTC is often used to synchronize tape recorders to MIDI based sequencers via SMPTE-to-MTC converters.

MIDI Thru Box A device which splits the data it receives at its MIDI In into two or more MIDI Thru sockets. Thus a master instrument with one MIDI Out could simultaneously send its data to several slave instruments via a MIDI Thru box. This avoids daisy chaining instruments together, simplifies the MIDI network and cuts down on possible timing problems.

MMC See MIDI Machine Control.

Mode See MIDI Mode.

Modulation In electronic musical instruments, 'modulation' refers to a vibrato effect which can be applied to the sound. The intensity of this modulation or vibrato is usually controlled by the modulation wheel found on the control panel. Modulation is transmitted via MIDI and is specified as MIDI Controller 1.

MROS Acronym for MIDI Real Time Operating System. Operating system developed by Steinberg to manage complex MIDI software systems where timing considerations are a priority.

MTC See MIDI Time Code

Multi-timbral Refers to the ability of a synthesizer or module to produce several different sounds at the same time controlled on different MIDI channels. Rather like a collection of synthesizers in one box.

Note Off In MIDI based music, a Note Off message describes the action of releasing a key on a musical keyboard. In other words, it terminates a musical event. It contains information about the pitch of the note to be switched off and the velocity with which the key was released.

Note On In MIDI based music a Note On message describes the action of pressing a key on a musical keyboard. In other words it starts the sounding of a musical event. It contains information about the pitch and the velocity of the note. Note On messages with a velocity of zero turn the note off in exactly the same way as the Note Off message (see above).

Pan Refers to the panoramic position of a sound within the stereo image. Most MIDI devices with two or more audio outputs are able to place each sound in the mix according to a pan control. The pan information is also usually sent and received via MIDI as Controller 10 thus allowing, for example, the control of the stereo mix from an external sequencer.

Patch In electronic musical instruments a 'patch' describes the configuration of the synthesis part of the instrument which creates a specific sound. Also referred to as program, voice, sound or preset. Each patch can usually be stored in the instrument's memory (see also Program Change).

Pitch Bend The continuous variation of the pitch of a sounding note. It is similar to the action of bending a note on a guitar. It is transmitted via MIDI as Pitch Bend messages and on electronic keyboard instruments it is usually controlled by a pitch wheel to the left of the keyboard.

Program Change A type of MIDI message used to remotely change the program number or 'patch' in a MIDI device. It can select program numbers between 0 – 127 and is transmitted on any of the 16 MIDI channels. Many MIDI devices do not follow a strictly logical arrangement for the location of sounds, which are often found in banks of 8, 32 or 64.

Quantize A term used in hardware and software sequencers to describe the action of automatically moving recorded notes onto the nearest fraction of a bar according to a quantize value. For example, using a quantize value of 16 (meaning 1/16 notes or semiquavers) will shift all inaccurately played notes onto the nearest 1/16 division of the bar.

While this is useful for correcting inaccurate playing it can also produce undesirably robotic music. The more advanced sequencers provide several different methods of quantizing material. These include the ability to move notes 'towards' a quantize value according to a percentage value and moving notes according to a pre-recorded 'feel' template.

Real-time Recording music into a sequencer in real-time simply means that the actual performance as it is played is what is recorded, much like recording onto a tape recorder (see Step-time).

SMPTE Acronym for 'Society of Motion Picture and Television Engineers'. An American organisation responsible for setting film and audio standards and recommended practices. For convenience, time code is often referred to as 'SMPTE' (pronounced 'simptee') but, in fact, this is only one type of time code (see Time Code).

Song Position Pointer A MIDI message often included when synchronizing MIDI devices using MIDI timing clocks. It enables the slaved instrument to synchronize to the same position in the music as the master instrument. The user may therefore fast forward and rewind to any position in the song and, going into play mode, restart all units from the same bar in perfect synchronization. Most MIDI sequencers provide the option of transmitting and receiving MIDI clocks with Song position pointers, as do many drum machines.

'Song position pointer' is also a term used by Steinberg Cubase to refer to the vertical line in the Arrange window and editors marking the Song position. This is also known as the Song position triangle or indicator.

Step Time A method of entering notes into a sequencer one step at a time (also referred to as step Input). The pitch, position and duration for each entry is pre-determined and after input is complete the music can be played back at any tempo. Step time provides a useful method of entering notes into a sequencer when the passage to be played is either too fast or too complicated(see real-time).

Sustain Pedal MIDI Controller number 64 also known as the damper pedal. Used to produce the same effect as the sustain pedal on a piano and is either on or off.

SysEx See System Exclusive.

System Exclusive A type of MIDI message allowing non-standardised communication between MIDI devices. Used for the transfer of manufacturer specific System Exclusive and also Universal System Exclusive data. Manufacturer specific System Exclusive includes a unique ID for each manufacturing company and might be used to change or control almost any parameter in the receiving device as deemed appropriate by the manufacturer. Universal System Exclusive encompasses a number of more recent additions to the MIDI Specification including MIDI Machine Control, MIDI Show Control, Sample Dump Standard, MIDI File Dump, General MIDI On, General MIDI Off and other data.

Time Code A time encoded signal recorded onto audio or video tape for time and point location and synchronization purposes. Sometimes referred to as 'SMPTE' (pronounced 'simptee') but, in fact, SMPTE is only one standard, as used in the USA. The other is EBU time code as used in Europe. Time code is measured in the following format:hours : minutes : seconds : frames : subframes. There are three essential types:

- Longitudinal Time Code (LTC) – commonly used for audio work.
- Vertical Interval Time Code (VITC) – popular for video editing.
- MIDI Time Code (MTC) – a special kind of time code transmitted via MIDI.

Time code may vary in the number of frames per second for the encoded signal. This is known as the frame rate and could be one of the following:

24 fps – traditional 35mm film rate.
25 fps – the European standard for audio and video (EBU).
30 fps – USA standard for audio only work.
30 dfps – Rarely used 'drop frame' standard.
29.97 fps – USA television and video format.
29.97 dfps – used for colour video work in the USA

When greater accuracy is required, as in audio work, the frame is divided into 80 subframes. For audio work it is normal practice to use 25 fps in Europe and 30 fps in the USA.

Velocity Refers to the speed (or force) with which a key is pressed or released on an electronic keyboard instrument. In order to transmit velocity information via MIDI the keyboard must be 'velocity sensitive'. In other words, it must have been manufactured to detect changes in the speed with which its keys are struck. Normally, the harder a key is struck the louder it will become and the higher will be the velocity value sent out via MIDI. However, velocity might also be used to affect the brightness, vibrato, sustain or some other expressive element within the sound. These effects might be used individually or in any combination.

Velocity forms part of the actual MIDI note data, (the third byte of Note On and Note Off messages), and does not assume a separate MIDI data category like many other parameters. However, due to the importance of velocity in musical expression for accent, dynamics and effects, MIDI sequencers provide easy access to this element of the data (see Note On and Note Off).

Volume The volume of sounds can be regulated via MIDI using Control Change 7. This is usually referred to as Main Volume and is implemented on most MIDI devices.

Appendix

For those readers needing more technical details the following outlines the actual message contents for the most popular types of MIDI data, as outlined in the glossary. This list is by no means exhaustive, but provides most of the essentials. All messages are shown in hexadecimal notation.

Active Sensing
FEH – Active Sensing message. This single unchanging message is normally transmitted once every 300 ms and is the master instrument's way of saying 'I am still here'.

Aftertouch (Channel Pressure)
DnH, vvH – Aftertouch message.
DnH = Aftertouch status byte and MIDI channel number (n).
vvH = the amount of pressure applied (0 – 127).

Balance
BnH, 08H, vvH – Balance Controller message.
BnH = Control Change status byte and MIDI channel number (n).
08H = Balance Controller number (8).
vvH = Control Value (0 – 127).

Bank Select
Two consecutive messages.
Message 1 – BnH, 00H, vvH – Bank Select message MSB (most significant bit).
Message 2 – BnH, 20H, vvH – Bank Select message LSB (least significant bit).
BnH = Control Change status byte and MIDI channel number (n).
00H = indicates the first part of the Bank Select message (MSB).
20H = indicates the second part of the Bank Select message (LSB).
vvH = the Control Change value (0 – 127).

Breath Controller
BnH, 02H, vvH – Breath Controller Control Change message.
BnH = Control Change status byte and MIDI channel number (n).
02H = Breath Controller number (2).
vvH = control value (0 – 127).

Control Change

BnH, ccH, vvH – Control Change message.
BnH = the Control Change status byte and MIDI channel number (n).
ccH = the Controller number (0 – 127).
vvH = the Controller's value (0 – 127).

Expression

BnH, OBH, vvH – Expression Control Change message.
BnH = Control Change status byte and MIDI channel number (n).
OBH = Expression Controller number (11).
vvH = control Value (0 – 127).

Modulation

BnH, 01H, vvH – Modulation message.
BnH = Control Change status byte with MIDI channel number (n).
01H = the Modulation Controller number (1).
vvH = the control value.

Note On

9nH, kkH, vvH – Note On message.
9nH = the Note On status byte and MIDI channel number (n).
kkH = the key or note number (0 – 127).
vvH = the velocity with which the note was struck (0 – 127).

Note Off

8nH, kkH, vvH – Note Off message.
8nH = the Note Off status byte and MIDI channel number (n).
kkH = the note number to be terminated (0 – 127).
vvH = the velocity with which the note was released (0 – 127).

Pan

BnH, OAH, vvH – Pan message.
BnH = the Control Change status byte and MIDI channel Number (n).
OAH = the Pan Controller number (10).
vvH = the control value (0 – 127).

Pitch Bend

EnH, ffH, ccH – Pitch Bend message.
EnH = the Pitch Bend status byte and MIDI channel number (n).
ffH = a number between 0 – 127 for fine changes in pitch.
ccH = a number between 0 – 127 for coarse changes.

Program Change

CnH, ppH – Program Change message.
CnH = the Program Change status byte and MIDI channel number (n).
ppH = the program number (0 – 127).

Sustain Pedal
BnH, 40H, vvH – Sustain Pedal Control Change message.
BnH = Control Change status byte and MIDI channel number (n).
40H = Sustain Pedal Controller number (64).
vvH = control value (0 – 63 = Off, 64 – 127 = On).

System Exclusive
F0H, iiH, nnH – nnH, F7H – System Exlusive message.
F0H = System Exclusive status byte.
iiH = manufacturer ID number (0 – 127).
nnH – nnH = Almost any sequence of data dependent on the function of
the message.
F7H = The end of the SysEx message, referred to as EOX (End of System
Exclusive).

Volume
BnH, 07H, vvH – Main Volume message.
BnH = the Control Change status byte and MIDI channel number (n).
07H = the Controller number for Main Volume (7).
vvH = the value for the volume level (0 – 127).

Index

For all sequencer users!

Sequencer Secrets

Over 150 power tips for MIDI sequencer users

Ian Waugh

108 pp ★ 216 x 138 mm ★ illustrated
ISBN 1870775 37 6

- 29 hands on projects
- Unlease the full potential of your sequencer
- Suitable for all software sequencers
- Become a power user
- Section on troubleshooting

£8.95 inc P&P

The manual may tell you how your sequencer works, but Sequencer Secrets goes beyond any manual. In this concise, creative and intensely practical book, Ian Waugh explains how you can get the best from any software sequencer. It contains a collection of hints and tips acquired over many years of experience with a wide range of software sequencers. It explains how to master functions you may have previously ignored, how to use short cuts to speed up your work, and how to turn your sequencer from a recording tool into a creative music machine.

The book will show you how to:

Optimise your MIDI system ★ Create MIDI echoes ★ Create instant harmonies ★ Humanise your drum patterns ★ Use controller messages more effectively ★ Use quantisation more effectively ★ Create more realistic instrument parts ★ Program gate effects ★ Use sequences live

A troubleshooting section helps you track down MIDI anomalies like double notes, volume dropouts, stuck notes and instruments going out of tune.

'Indispensable' *Future Music*
'Packed with helpful hints' *Sound on Sound*

Order hotline 01732 770893

PC Publishing
Tel 01732 770893 • Fax 01732 770268
email pcp@cix.compulink.co.uk
website http://www.pc-pubs.demon.co.uk

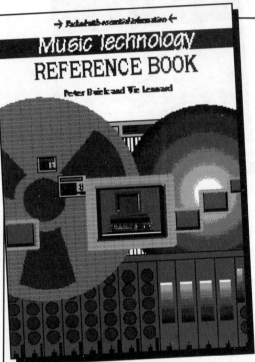

Basique

YOUR INVITATION TO JOIN – CLUB CUBASE UK

What is CCUK?
CCUK members receive a unique bi-monthly magazine (Basique) containing articles and news about Steinberg products and other related software, hardware, and equipment.

The right mix
Basique contains information about how to use Cubase and other products in the studio, on the road, and even in your bedroom!

We look in depth at MIDI and audio recording. How to make that 'brass section' sound real for example. There are introductions on how to use and set up the many various features in the whole range of Steinberg programs.

Computer gurus
We bring you technical news covering all three computer platforms (Atari, Apple Macintosh and Windows PCs).

Cubase user hints and tips pour off the pages to enable you to be more proficient and save time. We cover both MIDI and audio type information. 'I never knew that' well you will now.

New products
As in common with most computer software houses Steinberg are constantly updating and releasing new product. Basique provides you with information (a version chart) so that you can obtain the latest software updates. The magazine gives you full information on how to obtain that vital software update many of which only require a nominal handling charge.

How to save your money
Still not interested? Well what if we told you that you will be entitled to special offers and products and that you will enjoy up to 15% discount on all future Steinberg products that you buy! Even if you never read the magazine save yourself some money by joining Club Cubase. To be a member costs only £18.00 UK (£25.00 sterling overseas) for a year's membership. For further details contact us at:

Club Cubase
PO Box 11595
London SE26 4XE

E–mail: m2m@dircon.co.uk